Praise for Honey from the Rock
A Study of the Gospel of Grace.

I still remember it so vividly, that spring and summer of 1995. I thought my world was falling apart and I felt as if I were dying a little more each day. Looking back, I now know it was far more than the death of my mother, or our daughter's news about the complications about her pregnancy. No, it was not my world, it was me - *I* was falling apart. A lifetime of trying to be good enough, to live up to all the hopes, dreams and expectations of others; most of all my self-deceit which said that I had, in fact, been doing a rather wonderful job-- all this came crashing down on my head. Then a mentor of grace arrived, by the glorious providence of God. He helped me see I was not falling apart; rather, he opened to me the scriptures (and I had been a Bible major in college, and gone to seminary), showing me that the old Adamic Man I was carrying around, dressed up in religious garb, saying all the right things, doing all the right things, was truly a dead rotting corpse. Wow! Thanks for the Bad News, Mac! But, thanks be to God, Mac did not stop there. He turned the page in those scriptures and unfolded before my very eyes glorious Good News I had heard a thousand times before, but which was always filtered through my striving religious flesh, and which had not hit me with force and power. But now, having embraced my death, with stench like a four day dead Lazarus, I heard Jesus cry with a loud voice, "Mark, come forth!" Thank you, Mac, for faithfully preaching and teaching the true Gospel. Reading this book, or to use your image, going through these "family pictures," brings those glorious truths back with fresh power. Thanks, my friend, for helping to take off the grave clothes in which I'd been stumbling all those years.

Mark Smith, PhD; Professor of History,
Indiana Wesleyan University

HONEY FROM THE ROCK
A Study of the Gospel of Grace

*But I would feed you from the finest of wheat, and
with honey from the rock I would satisfy you.*
—Psalm 81:16

MAC GODDARD

*But I do not consider my life of any account as dear
to myself, in order that I may finish my course and the
ministry which I received from the Lord Jesus, to testify
solemnly of the gospel of the grace of God.*
—Acts 20:24

iUniverse LLC
Bloomington

HONEY FROM THE ROCK
A STUDY OF THE GOSPEL OF GRACE

Unless otherwise noted, all scripture quotations are taken from the New American Standard Bible (NASB) © 1960, 1962, 1963, 1968, 1971, 1972, 1973, 1975, 1977 and 1995 by the Lockman Foundation.

iUniverse books may be ordered through booksellers or by contacting:

iUniverse
1663 Liberty Drive
Bloomington, IN 47403
www.iuniverse.com
1-800-Authors (1-800-288-4677)

ISBN: 978-1-4917-1874-2 (sc)
ISBN: 978-1-4917-1876-6 (hc)
ISBN: 978-1-4917-1875-9 (e)

Library of Congress Control Number: 2013923002

Printed in the United States of America.

iUniverse rev. date: 12/13/2013

How blessed is the one whom Thou dost choose, and bring near to Thee, to dwell in Thy courts. We will be satisfied with the goodness of Thy house, Thy holy temple.

–Psalm 65:4

With more love than I could ever express to them, I dedicate this brief theological treatise to my children, Amy Goddard Butler and Michael Brannen Goddard, and to my grandchildren, Sydney Michele Ray and Caroline Ashley Ray. I do so praying that the one, true gospel will grip their hearts as it has mine.

To all of those whom God foreknew, predestined,
called, justified, and glorified—
those whose names are written
in the Lamb's Book of Life.

To Him be glory forever! Amen!

CONTENTS

PREFACE

For me, writing is always a work in progress. I write and rewrite and write some more and rewrite again. For some reason, God gave me a mind that requires that I make sure anything I put into print about the gospel fits into the larger picture of the gospel. That means I have to read and reread to make certain I am not adulterating the gospel. For example, in one paragraph I might declare that salvation is by grace alone through faith alone in Jesus alone but on another page imply there are things we must do to earn salvation. In my mind, I must not allow that to happen. Actually, most of the time the differences are much more subtle than in the example I just gave you, so I really have to be on guard. As you might imagine, this same kind of scrutiny is true concerning the title of whatever I might be writing.

Several days ago, a dear friend of mine, Lynn Reece from Louisville, Kentucky, called to ask me to come to Louisville to teach a group of couples over a long weekend. Of course, I readily agreed, and we continued to talk about the possibilities for that weekend. To put it mildly, I was excited, more than I have been in a very long time. To tell you the truth, I even had a difficult time going to sleep that night, as my mind was racing with excitement. Anyway, one afternoon, a day or so later, I was taking a nap when the Holy Spirit spoke to me. I sat upright in bed and wide awake. This is what He said: "Honey from the Rock!" I immediately got my Bible and looked up Psalm 81, where those words are located.

When I read that Psalm, I knew I had the theme for the weekend in Louisville. I immediately called Lynn, and she agreed. The next day, the Holy Spirit quietly said, *"Honey from the Rock* is also the title for your book." Please understand that I very seldom indicate that the Holy Spirit has spoken so clearly to me.

The context of the text is quite simple. Israel was living in disobedience to God, so He was encouraging them to turn from their disobedience and to walk in His ways. It is important that you remember that Israel was living under the covenant of law; consequently, disobedience was the way of life for them—the only way. As we know, to walk in His ways they, like Abraham, would have had to put their faith in Jesus rather than in the law. God promised that, should they walk in His ways, He would, among other things, satisfy them with "honey from the rock."

As you know, a rock is hard—"hard as a rock!" In this life, there is no more difficult (hard!) place than the place Israel found themselves—trying to live in obedience to God in their own strength; trying to live in relationship with God as a result of obedience to the law. To be sure, they would never enjoy honey from the rock while living in this condition of self-righteousness.

Sadly, most modern-day churchgoers are living the very same way the Israelites were living—trying to please God through obedience to the law (or someone's interpretation of it). God did not approve of that then, and neither does He approve of it now. In my opinion, the same promise applies today, even though He made it to the Israelites of old. If we will walk in His ways, trusting in Jesus and in Jesus alone, He will not only feed us with the finest of wheat but also satisfy us with honey from the rock. In other words, on the other side of that extremely difficult place created by the old covenant of law, He will nourish us with the sweetest of honey— *honey from the rock.*

As you know, God identified the land of Canaan, the Promised Land, the land on the other side of the wilderness wanderings, as a land of milk and honey. "So I have come down to deliver them from the power of the Egyptians and to bring them up from that land to a good and spacious land, to a land flowing with milk and honey" (Exodus 3:8). Sadly, it took them forty years to make a ten-day journey. Sadly, I know many modern-day churchgoers who are yet wandering in the wilderness of self-righteousness.

This is why, in my mind, the only thing that is as important as understanding the one, true gospel—the gospel of the Grace of God—is teaching it to others. As a result of that mind-set, I have pretty much given my life to the study of this astonishing message. As you might imagine, as the Holy Spirit began to open my eyes and to give me a measure of understanding, He also stirred within me a desire to share with others what He was revealing to me—to teach the Gospel. Over the past thirty-five or so years, it has been my purpose to do just that.

At this point, I am seventy-one years old, and I am fully aware that I have already lived more years on this earth than I have left; consequently, I have a strong desire to put into print the heart and essence of what the Holy Spirit has, thus far, revealed to me. That might sound a bit strange to you, but for me, not doing so would be about like you reaching my age and deciding to burn all of your family pictures.

The message of the good news of Jesus—the One True Gospel— is far more precious to me than a house filled with my family pictures, and I might add, my family pictures *are* very precious to me.

For what it is worth, I have decided not to burn the "family pictures!" I have decided, instead, to attempt to scan them from my mind onto this paper and preserve them for whomever the Holy Spirit chooses.

Mac Goddard

ACKNOWLEDGMENTS

In September of 1960, my parents and I arrived at Asbury College in Wilmore, Kentucky, for me to begin my college journey. Daddy wanted me to attend his alma mater, Emory University, so Asbury was not his choice of schools for me. To put it mildly, he was not overjoyed. After a terrible lunch in the dining hall, which made matters worse, the three of us walked outside, where in the providence of God, we met Bobby Ray Martin, who was already an upperclassman and a true Southern boy. This meeting would prove to be one of those divine appointments. Martin, as I call him, took me under his wing (relieving my father of much stress and anxiety!), and within a day, I became his roommate in 101 Johnson Hall. Since that meeting, we have been very close friends. The truth is he became a family member. On her death bed, when my mother-in-law knew no one, not even her daughter, Martin walked up to her bedside and said, "Blanche, do you know who this is?" Her reply was quick and thoroughly like Blanche: "Course I do—Bobby Ray Martin!"

Because of our deep friendship, I asked him to read through the manuscript for this book and make any comments or corrections he saw fit. I even asked him to point out those places where he disagreed. As you might imagine, he readily agreed to do so and got the job done pronto. When he had finished, we sat together, and I listened as he walked me through his comments and suggestions. I can assure you that they made this book much more readable.

Martin, I want to thank you for being my true friend and for taking the time to read through the manuscript of this bit of theological rambling. If anyone's life is challenged because of this book, we will both rejoice and give all the praise to Him.

INTRODUCTION

I grew up in a very conservative (don't color outside the lines!) and a very legalistic (keep all the rules!) environment. As you can imagine, my belief system was not my own; it belonged to those significant others who were influencing my life. Fortunately, I finally reached the place where I realized I actually had a mind and could think for myself, and doing so was quite liberating for me and very fine with God!

Unfortunately, during that time, I became completely convinced that pleasing God, gaining His acceptance, being blessed while here on this earth, and getting to heaven were all wrapped up in my behavior. In other words, for me, Christianity was very me-centered and performance based. Of course, keeping the Ten Commandments was absolutely essential, not to mention the rules of conduct that were imposed on me by certain significant others, who felt free to interpret those Ten Commandments as they saw fit (albeit, well intentioned, I am sure).

Fortunately, sin, thinking it was doing one thing, played right into the hands of the Holy Spirit. What Satan meant for harm, God used for good! How? Sin used the holy law of God to deceive me into believing I would find life through my obedience; however (to use the words of Paul), when the law came, sin became alive and I died. My death, however, was a good thing—a very good thing! How so? It was the man I was in Adam that died (i.e., I died to my own efforts to find life through my obedience). The tree of knowledge of good and evil and I parted company. Actually, the law, along with all the aforementioned interpretations, proved to be a schoolmaster, a child trainer that drove me, in utter desperation, to Jesus. It took a while for Him to purge my mind of all the stuff I held "sacred" (my mind really did need renewing), but He finally gave me eyes to see! Since then, I have not been able to get enough of the gospel for myself, nor have I grown tired of teaching these truths to others. It really is the passion of my life.

That said, it is important that I tell you of an epiphany I had many years ago as I was reading Paul's letter to the church at Galatia. This is what I read:

> I am amazed that you are so quickly deserting Him who called you by the grace of Christ, for a different gospel; which is really not another; only there are some who are disturbing you, and want to distort the gospel of Christ. But even though we, or an angel from heaven, should preach to you a gospel contrary to that which we have preached to you, let him be accursed. As we have said before, so I say again now, if any man is preaching to you a gospel contrary to that which you received, let him be accursed. (Galatians 1:6–9)

In my mind, those were pretty strong words—words most would perceive as coming from an arrogant know-it-all. Who in their right mind would make such a statement? What sincere preacher would ever declare, especially in a letter, that the gospel he preaches is not only the only true gospel but also that anyone who disagrees and preaches another should be eternally separated from God? Notice that Paul not only included himself but also angels from heaven!

An even more significant question is this: Why did God include these comments from Paul in the scriptures? In my mind, the answer is obvious. He wanted to make these two things very clear: (1) there is but one gospel, and it is the one Paul preached; and (2) to preach another is anathema. That answer led to my epiphany, which was this: I should be certain that the gospel I preach is in fact the gospel Paul preached.

My theology is far removed from that which so influenced my early life. When I finally realized I could think for myself, I also realized I did not have to fit into anybody's pigeonhole! I am simply a man who continues to seek to know the one, true gospel and to preach it as God provides opportunity.

After my epiphany, I stopped reading the Bible in an effort to make it fit into someone's theological position, even my own. I read it now to know Him, whom to know is eternal life—*period*! I am simply in search of truth—the truth that is the person of Jesus Christ, who is, in fact, the good news!

I really think Paul expressed my true feelings when he said this: "But I do not consider my life of any account as dear to myself, in order that I may finish my course, and the ministry which I received from the Lord Jesus, to testify solemnly of the gospel of the grace of God" (Acts 20:24).

Mac Goddard
August 2013

1

CREATION

The story of creation is one of the most breathtaking in the entire Bible. Take a minute and picture God looking out over a vast emptiness, a limitless void, and then listen as one by one He calls into being that which does not exist! Whatever His mouth speaks immediately steps out on the stage of nothingness and is. What an awesome picture! Listen carefully to the sounds of creation.

God said, "Let there be light" *and there was light.* (Genesis 1:3)

God said, "Let there be an expanse in the midst of the waters and let it separate the waters from the waters"; *and it was so.* (Genesis 1:6–7)

God said, "Let the waters below the heavens be gathered into one place, and let the dry land appear"; *and it was so.* (Genesis 1:9)

God said, "Let the earth sprout vegetation, plants yielding seed, and fruit trees bearing fruit after their kind, with seed in them, on the earth"; *and it was so.* (Genesis 1:11)

God said, "Let there be lights in the expanse of the heavens to separate the day from the night, and let them be for signs, and for seasons, and for days and years; and let them be for lights in the expanse of the heavens to give light on the earth"; *and it was so.* (Genesis 1:14–15)

God said, "Let the earth bring forth living creatures after their kind: cattle and creeping things and beasts of the earth after their kind"; *and it was so.* (Genesis 1:24)

Then God Said, "Let Us make man in Our own image, according to Our likeness; and let them rule over the fish of the sea and over the birds of the sky and over the cattle and over all the earth, and over every creeping thing that creeps on the earth." And God created man in His own image, in the image of God He created him; male and female He created them. And God blessed them; and God said to them, "Be fruitful and multiply, and fill the earth, and subdue it; and rule over the fish of the sea and over the birds of the sky, and over every living thing that moves on the earth." *(*Genesis 1:26–28)

God saw all that He had made, and behold, it was very good. (Genesis 1:31)

Man, created in the image of the Father, Son, and Holy Spirit (Genesis 1:26), according to their likeness (Genesis 1:26), with God's stamp of approval placed upon him (Genesis 1:31), finds himself in perfect relationship with God! No sin. No shame. No hiding. No reason to hide. Just perfect, beautiful intimacy with the Father and with the Son and with the Holy Spirit! That is how it was *in the beginning*!

If, for whatever reason, you cannot accept the fact that God literally created *everything*, and that He did so from absolutely *nothing*, then sadly, you will be unable to accept the one, true gospel—the gospel of the grace of God.

Eugene Peterson, in *The Message*, said this:

> First, God. God is the subject of life. God is foundational for living. If we don't have a sense of the primacy of God, we will never get it right, get life right, get our lives right. Not God at the margins; not God as an option; not God on the weekends. God at center and circumference; God first and last: God, God, God.[1]

You see, the gospel is the story of the God of creation doing an even greater miracle than the miracle of physical creation. It is the story of His creating from nothing, a new creation in Christ Jesus! "Therefore if any man is in Christ, he is a new creature; the old things have passed away; behold, new things have come" (2 Corinthians 5:1)

This new creation, this redeemed individual, did not exist, until God spoke him into existence. "In Him we have redemption through His blood, the forgiveness of our trespasses, according to the riches of His grace, which He lavished upon us" (Ephesians 1:7–8a). "For you have been born again not of seed which is perishable but imperishable, that is, through the living and abiding word of God" (1 Peter 1:2) And by the way, God did this speaking from the foundation of the world. "He finished His works from the foundation of the world" (Hebrews 4:3b). Do not allow that to throw you off. Just keep reading—please.

---

[1]   Eugene H. Peterson, *The Message*, 19.

Questions for Study

1. Describe how things were for Adam and Eve as they lived in the garden before the fall.

2. Why is it critically important that you accept the fact of creation?

3. Which is the greater miracle, the miracle of physical creation or the miracle of the new creation?

4. When did the new creation's existence begin?

2

FIRST ADAM—FIRST MAN

Then the Lord God formed man of the dust from the ground, and breathed into his nostrils the breath of life; and man became a living being. (Genesis 2:7— the *first* Adam and *first* man)

The truth is we know very little about God. I suppose He designed it so; after all, it was His decision for Him to be the Father and for us to be His children. Somehow, He had a committee meeting with Himself (Father, Son, and Holy Spirit) and decided He would be the potter and we would be the clay. In other words, He decided He would choose what He would reveal of Himself in us and to us and through us, as we merely rest on the Potter's wheel. We will simply have to get along without what He chose not to reveal; after all, being His child is a life of faith.

Thankfully, He did choose to make some things about Himself known. For example, He chose to reveal to us that He is love. "And we have come to know and have believed the love which God has for us. God is love, and the one who abides in love abides in God, and God abides in Him" (1 John 4:16).

With that revelation, we are confronted with this problem: it is very difficult for us to grasp the concept of love because it is so very slippery. For example, one might say, "I *love* fried chicken." Another might say, "I *love* deer hunting." Another might say, "I *love* my mother." One might even say, "I *love* my enemies." Someone might dare even to say, "I *love* sinners." One would surely say, "I *love* my wife!" In addition, let us not forget that there would be those brave souls who would say, "I love God!" To be sure, there would be the few who would have the courage to say, "God loves me!"

As you can see, in each of these examples, the word *love* is very slippery. About the time you think you have it figured out, the meaning changes! It is one thing to say, "I *love* fried chicken," but it is quite another to say, "God *loves* me!" Even so, God declares that He is love! God is whatever love is in its highest and purest form! To tell you the truth, I doubt it has much to do with fried chicken, even though I truly believe He would "love" it.

God also chose to reveal to us that He is holy. Maybe Isaiah said it best: "Holy, Holy, Holy is the Lord of hosts" (Isaiah 6:3). In other words, God is not simply holy; He is thrice holy, as in holy, holy, holy!

Again, however, that revelation presents us with this problem: we know less about holiness than we know about love! On one hand, what we have seen done in the name of love has so distorted our concept of love that most of us run from whatever it is; however, on the other hand, holiness is so foreign to us that, for the most part, we do not have a clue as to what it is. The truth is I do not believe the Israelites of old had a clue. They used the word often, but what they were referring to was some religious "something" that was, at best, only a shadow of true holiness. The fact is this: self-righteous religion and holiness, like light and darkness, simply cannot coexist.

I must tell you that most of what I learned early on about holiness had nothing to do with true holiness; in fact, it was not even a shadow of holiness! Much like the Jews, I learned that holiness was not only something I was supposed to do but also something I was supposed to earn and evidence by my obedience. It was so me-centered that it really had nothing to do with God. From my frame of reference, holiness had more to do with such notions as keeping boys and girls from swimming in the same pool together than it ever had to do with God. Simply put, if it was fun, it was not holy. Tragically, I was convinced that I was having fun by attempting to follow these rules, and even more tragically, I was also convinced that I was pretty good at following them. Now you know why I love the picture of Jesus laughing that hangs on my office wall. What a relief!

What can we say then? We can say that whatever else love might be, it is first and foremost the stuff of which God is made, and we can say He demonstrated it to us on the cross when He did not spare His own Son but delivered Him up for us. "But God demonstrated His own love toward us, in that while we were yet sinners, Christ died for us" (Romans 5:8). "He who did not spare His own Son, but delivered Him up for us all, how will He not also with Him freely give us all things?" (Romans 8:32). "Love never fails!" (1 Corinthians 13:8).

In addition, we can say that whatever else holiness might be, it also is first and foremost the stuff of which God is made, and we can say He demonstrated His holiness to us when He required that His Son bear our sins in His body on the cross. "And He Himself bore our sins in His body on the cross, that we might die to sin and live to righteousness; for by His wounds you were healed" (1 Peter 2:24). Holiness never compromises!

Now, think ahead a bit and ask yourself this question: What would a God of love and holiness do with His love and holiness? Would He just sit around in heaven saying, "I am love and holiness"? I think not! The answer seems so obvious to me, especially in light of the fact that I have hindsight. He would create man and place within him the need for His love and holiness, and furthermore, He would place man in an environment that was drenched with His love and holiness.

Why would He do these things? On the one hand, He would want man to be eager to *receive* His love and holiness, to be the recipient of who He is. On the other hand, He would not want him to be exposed to sin! Ultimately, of course, He did both of these to glorify Himself!

The obvious proof is this: "And God said, 'Let Us make man in Our image, according to our likeness ...'" (Genesis 1:26). "Then the Lord God formed man of dust from the ground, and breathed into his nostrils the breath of life; and man became a living soul" (Genesis 2:7). "And God saw all that He had made, and behold, it was very good" (Genesis 1:31). What an incredible picture: the first Adam, first man, living in perfect relationship with God!

That, however, is not the end of the creation of the first Adam. Thankfully, God saw it was not good for man to live alone! "Then the Lord God said, 'It is not good for the man to be alone; I will make him a helper suitable for him'" (Genesis 2:18). God saw that man was not complete, and He did what only God could do:

> So the Lord God caused a deep sleep to fall upon the man, and he slept; then He took one of his ribs, and closed up the flesh at that place. And the Lord God fashioned into a woman the rib that He had taken from the man, and brought her to the man. ... This is now bone of my bones, and flesh of my flesh. (Genesis 2:21–23)

She was the rest of him! The first Adam, first man—complete—and in a perfect and holy love relationship with each other and with God!

Listen to this illustration from Michael Horton's book *We Believe*:

> Imagine a friend telling you that she has fallen in love with a man she has known for some time now. For weeks she has been mutely staring right through you, as if the fellow's face were projected on the wall behind you. Finally, she runs up to you as you are returning from shopping, nearly knocking the groceries out of your arms. "I'm in love!" she announces. "We're getting married!" During all of this time, however, you have continually asked her about this man. What

is he like? What does he do? Where is he from? Who are his parents? But all you get are the blank stares. "I don't know," she finally answers. "I don't want to know about him; I just want to know him."[2]

As I said, we know very little about God; however, we can know Him, even as Adam and Eve knew Him in the beginning.

Questions for Study

1. Why do you suppose we know so little about God?

2. Thankfully, God chose to make two things about Himself very clear. What were they?

3. I indicated that we have a problem with love. What is it?

4. I indicated that we have a problem with holiness. What is it?

5. Define love.

6. Define holiness.

---

[2]   Michael Scott Horton, *We Believe; Recovering the Essentials of the Apostle's Creed* (Nashville, TN: Word Publishing, 1998), 28.

7. What would the God of love and holiness do with His love and holiness?

8. Why would this God of love and holiness do the above-mentioned things?

9. Why did God choose to bring Eve on the scene?

3

THE FALL

Was this "first Adam, first man" really complete? He was living in a perfect place, in a perfect relationship with God and with his wife! God's instructions to him were very clear, easy, and *uncomplicated*: Be fruitful and multiply; rule over everything that moves; and eat from any tree that you like—any tree, that is, except the tree of knowledge of good and evil. *Do not eat the fruit of that tree,* for in the day that you do you will die (see Genesis 1:26–28, 2:16–17). Notice that He gave them only one thou-shalt-not rule—one No Trespassing sign!

The following is a quote from Craig Barnes's book *Searching for Home: Spirituality for Restless Souls*:

> It is striking that the creation narratives make a point of telling us that this forbidden fruit was in the midst of the garden and not off in some forgettable corner. This means we were created to live with an unavoidable reminder that home was never meant to be perfect, whole, or complete. That's God's idea of a good creation. What was missing from the good garden was meant to serve as our altar of prayer, where we could bend our knees and confess that we were mere creatures who were never meant to have it

all, but were dependent on our Creator, who alone is
whole and complete. That pristine, sacred communion
was precisely what made the garden so good.[3]

Let's think about this often-missed but terribly important detail:
God purposely placed the forbidden fruit tree in the middle of
the garden, right where Adam and Eve would see it all day and be
tempted by its relentless attractiveness. They could hardly pass by it
without being drawn by its power. Without their even being aware
of it, the tree of life was becoming less and less attractive and the tree
of knowledge of good and evil was increasing in its attractiveness.

At this point, it is important that we remember that God does
not tempt us to sin—period.

> Let no one say when he is tempted, "I am being
> tempted by God"; for God cannot be tempted by evil,
> and He Himself does not tempt anyone. But each one
> is tempted when he is carried away and enticed by his
> own lust. Then when lust has conceived, it gives birth
> to sin; and when sin is accomplished, it brings forth
> death. (James 1:15)

Obviously, God was *not* tempting Adam and Eve to sin; instead,
He was encouraging them to righteousness. He was making them
aware that, even in this good and perfect garden, they must live in
absolute dependence upon Him (the fleshing out of righteousness)
and not themselves (the fleshing out of religion). Interestingly, after
providing them with perfect instructions, He gave them the freedom
to choose which road they preferred—dependence or independence—
and He did so knowing they would choose independence. In other
words, their choice was within the parameters of God's providence.

---

[3]   M. Craig Barnes, *Searching for Home: Spiritually for Restless Souls* (Grand
Rapids, MI: Brazos Press 2003), 13–14

Enter the Serpent—Satan Himself

As you know, Satan *is* the deceiver, the one who tempts us to sin, and he is relentless in his mission. Adam and Eve would not escape his prowess; sadly, they became his first two victims.

The following is what Satan said in his effort to deceive Adam and Eve: "Indeed, has God said, 'You shall not eat from any tree of the garden? … You surely shall not die! God knows that in the day you eat from it your eyes will be opened, and you will be like God, knowing good and evil'" (Genesis 3:1b, 4–5). As you know, his ploy worked, and this first man, along with his wife, chose independence over dependence.

To the untrained eye, it appears that this forbidden fruit made this good garden anything but good—imperfect and incomplete. The mind-set probably went something like this: there is something more, something better, and God is keeping it from us, but we desperately want it!

Hold on a minute, however, and take a more careful look. This forbidden fruit is exactly what made this good garden perfect. You see, *there is no perfection outside of dependence upon Him.* Surely, Adam's and Eve's choice to pursue the route of the knowledge of good and evil evidences this.

As you remember, this forbidden fruit was not an "apple of gold" that God was hiding from them, the eating of which would make them like God and thereby complete what was missing. Instead, it was a system of rules that would generate a lifestyle of independence from God, a lifestyle that said, "We not only can know what is good and evil, but we can also perfectly perform the good and avoid the evil and thereby please You by our works"—legalism, the fruit of independence, at its finest hour!

Yes, most of us know *now* that God was not trying to hide some good thing from this first couple by placing this forbidden fruit tree in the middle of this good garden; instead, He was giving them an opportunity to avoid the most tragic of mistakes—attempting to live life independently of Him.

Sadly, most of those who attend Christian churches today live (because they have been taught to do so) as if the tree of knowledge of good and evil is firmly planted right in the center of their sanctuaries, and sadly, it is just as attractive today as it was in the garden, even more so. It is because we really do believe we can make it on our own, maybe with a bit of God's help along the way, but for the most part, we can go it on our own.

Now, I really want you to see this, so please look carefully: as long as the tree of knowledge of good and evil stood in the good garden, the garden was imperfect by God's design, *or so it seems*; after all, He purposely placed it there. However, as strange as it might seem, *that* piece of *imperfection*—not only believing we can know good and evil but also believing we can perform the good and avoid the evil—is *the very thing* that drives us to that which is perfect, namely, Jesus, the tree of life. This is what Paul had to say about that: "Therefore the Law has become our tutor [child trainer] to lead us to Christ, that we may be justified by faith. But now that faith has come, we are no longer under a tutor" (Galatians 3:24–25; brackets mine).

Paradoxically, this tells us that the forbidden fruit tree had a prefect purpose after all because it accomplished God's purpose— the leading of His elect to a life of utter dependence upon Him—and this is a very good thing—a perfect thing!

It is somewhat ironic that God places the very things we try so hard to hide from other Christians—things that cause them to stumble—right out in the middle of everywhere, so they will stumble, yet not so as to fall headlong but into His embrace and security. "The steps of a man are established by the Lord; and He delights in his way. When he falls, he shall not be hurled headlong; because the Lord is the One who holds his hand" (Psalm 37:23–24 NASB).

It is important for you to realize that *at this point*, neither Adam nor Eve had eaten from the tree of life, and neither had they eaten from the tree of knowledge of good and evil, which just might indicate they were about to make the only free choice man has ever made. (They were under the influence of neither tree.)

So what happened? Adam chose to do what every man would choose to do when he has a free choice; he made the wrong choice! He chose to do the *only* thing God told him not to do! He ate the fruit of the tree of knowledge of good and evil. He made the very same choice each one of us would have made had we been there (and we were)—the wrong choice! The truth is this first Adam, first man disregarded God's simple, straightforward directive and chose what *seemed* best to him. After all, "it was good for food, it was a delight to the eyes, and it was desirable to make one wise" (Genesis 3:6), not to mention that it had a No Trespassing sign nailed to its trunk, which is really what made it so desirable.

As you know, there were two significant trees in the middle of the garden: the tree of knowledge of good and evil and the tree of life (Genesis 2:9). When given the choice, this "first Adam, first man" chose the tree of knowledge of good and evil, and in doing so, he rejected the tree of life—Jesus. Apart from Him, man is altogether incomplete; in fact, he is completely helpless and hopeless! How thankful I am that He can call into existence things that are not!

Let us take a careful look at just how this fall came about. What really happened? We see man, created in the image of God, living it up in the garden of Eden, doing what he likes best—ruling over every living thing! Actually, there was only one problem, one difficulty. The be-fruitful-and-multiply rule was easy enough; the rule-over-everything rule was actually quite exhilarating; and the eat-from-any-tree-of-the-garden rule was very attractive. However, it was the thou-shalt-not rule that was the problem. "And the Lord God commanded the man, saying, 'From any tree of the Garden you may eat freely; but from the tree of knowledge of good and evil *you shall not eat,* for in the day that you eat from it you shall surely die'" (Genesis 2:16–17, emphasis mine). Somehow, thou-shalt-not rules just go against the grain; they make their objects so alluring! I am certain that you know how No Trespassing signs affect you! The other swimming and fishing holes are never as attractive as the ones with the No Trespassing signs! I have the strong feeling that this is why the Holy Spirit caused Paul to pen these words: "The sting of death is sin, and the power of sin is the law" (1 Corinthians 15:56). "For apart from the Law sin is dead" (Romans 7:8).

At any rate, here is the story. "Now the serpent was more crafty than any beast of the field which the Lord God had made" (Genesis 3:1). I can understand where that might be a bit intimidating to the uninformed, but God had certainly informed Adam! He told him to rule over everything that moves in the sky and on the earth, which included the serpent! To tell you the truth, I really think Adam's choice had more to do with the No Trespassing sign than it did with the serpent, and I think the serpent knew that. After all, he is crafty!

As any crafty one would do, the serpent asked Eve, not Adam, this question: "Indeed, has God said, 'You shall not eat from any tree of the garden'?" (Genesis 3:1). The truth is the serpent knew what God had said, and so did Eve. I might add, they both knew this was not what He had said. His purpose should have been obvious: he wanted Eve to begin questioning what God had said so she would become confused about it. After all, he is the author of confusion!

Her response, however, was *fairly* accurate: "From the fruit of the trees in the garden we may eat; but from the fruit of the tree which is in the middle of the garden, God has said, 'You shall not eat of it or touch it, lest you die'" (Genesis 3:2–3)! I indicated that her response was only *fairly* accurate because God never said anything about not *touching* the tree. Yes, that might be implied; but the fact is, Eve misquoted God! It does not seem like a very significant thing, but then, misquoting God never does, especially in the middle of temptation.

The serpent accomplished his first mission: deception and confusion! He was using that good, holy, and righteous No Trespassing sign (the thou-shalt-not rule) to bring about deception and confusion. Using that which is good, holy, and righteous (the law) to bring about deception, confusion, and ultimately death would prove to be his long-term course of action.

What shall we say then? Is the Law sin? May it never be! On the contrary, I would not have come to know sin except through the Law; for I would not have known about coveting if the Law had not said, "You shall not covet." But sin taking opportunity through the commandment, produced in me coveting of every kind; for apart from the Law sin is dead. And I was once alive apart from the Law; but when the commandment came, sin became alive and I died; and this commandment, which was to result in life, proved to result in death for me; for sin, taking opportunity through the commandment, deceived me, and through it killed me. So then, the Law is holy, and the commandment is holy and righteous and good. Therefore did that which is good become a cause of death for me? May it never be! Rather it was sin, in order that if might be shown to be sin by effecting my death through that which is good, that through the commandment sin might become utterly sinful. For we know that the Law is spiritual; but I am of flesh, sold into bondage to sin. (Romans 7:7–14)

Jim McNeely had something to say about this in his book *The Romance of Grace*. Please pay careful attention to it:

It bears saying that what the law really does is press notions of right and wrong on the unwilling person, setting him against his desires. The law insists on the moral good, even though the inner desire is for the forbidden. This is the heartbeat of what is variously called "legalism" or "pharisaism."[4]

---

[4]   Jim McNeely, *The Romance of Grace* (Seattle: Vox Dei, 2013), 23.

Now, watch how the deception and confusion increase! "And the serpent said to the woman, 'You surely shall not die!'" (Genesis 3:4). Have you ever wondered why the serpent did not question Eve's comment about not touching the tree? It should be obvious: he thrives on deception and confusion. Sometimes what he fails to do is just as significant as what he does. Anyway, he now makes an all-out effort to convince Eve that God is a liar: *You surely shall not die!*

To be sure, Eve knew what God had said, and she also knew He was no liar; consequently, she knew death would be the result of eating the fruit of the tree of knowledge of good and evil. The serpent, however, knew just how easy it would be to deceive her, and he was on a no-holds-barred, all-out mission to deceive her just enough to get her to take one bite of the fruit from the forbidden tree, and he was because he knew that *that* would be all it would take.

Then the really big blow—"For God knows that in the day you eat from it your eyes will be opened, and you will be like God, knowing good and evil" (Genesis 3:5). In other words, so says the serpent (the deceiver), "God knows that the very best fruit comes from His tree, the tree of knowledge of good and evil and He obviously does not want you to eat from His tree!"

This might be closer to the way it really was: *God is trying to keep the good fruit from you because He knows that should you become like Him, you would no longer need Him. You could do this thing called life on your own, without having to depend upon Him! In other words, you could be independent! Essentially and effectively, the serpent was saying this: Do not listen to Him; listen to me. You can trust me, but you cannot trust Him.*

The tragic fall: "When the woman saw that the tree was good for food, and that it was a delight to the eyes, and that the tree was desirable to make one wise, she took from its fruit and ate; and she gave also to her husband with her, and he ate" (Genesis 3:6). *Note this*: At this point, both Adam and Eve had rejected the tree of life but had eaten of the fruit of the tree of knowledge of good and evil. That meant they could no longer make free choices! From that moment forward, they could make only sinful choices, as they were controlled by the influence of the tree of knowledge of good and evil.

Unfortunately, Eve bought the lie—lock, stock, and barrel— even though the No Trespassing sign was clearly visible on the trunk of the tree! Yes, they were convinced that the fruit of the tree was good for food, a delight to the eyes, and desirable to make one wise; however, the No Trespassing sign made it even more desirable! It actually aroused lust—passionate desire! "For while we were in the flesh, the sinful passions, which were aroused by the Law, were at work in the members of our body to bear fruit for death" (Romans 7:5).

Actually, the No Trespassing sign was not *the* problem because it was really a good and righteous sign! All it did was hang on the tree as a warning to those who came near. The truth is this: the serpent *used* the No Trespassing sign as an enticement because he knew that apart from the No Trespassing sign, lust (the bad kind) was dead! "But sin, taking opportunity through the commandment, produced in me coveting (lust) of every kind; for apart from the Law sin is dead" (Romans 7:8). You see, the problem was sin—the exceeding sinfulness of sin.

What was the fruit of this tragic fall? "Then the eyes of both of them were opened, and they knew that they were naked; and they sewed fig leaves together and made themselves loin coverings" (Genesis 3:7). Again, the serpent had it partially correct. The eyes of both of them *were* opened, but they did not become like God, not even close! Much to the contrary, they saw that they were naked, and for the very first time, they experienced shame—intense shame! Far, far from becoming like God, they became like the serpent— offensive to God.

This is what Merle Fossum and Marilyn Mason had to say, in the introduction of their book, about shame:

> This book is about a dragon, a mythic monster called same. Few people in our culture have escaped this

creature, whose claws can lock us in a frozen state and devour our ability to verbalize.[5]

Notice this line: "They knew that they were naked!" Can you believe this was the first time they had noticed their nakedness? How could one possibly live with another, especially someone of the opposite sex, and not even notice that he or she is naked? The answer should be obvious: Sin, especially self-righteousness, breeds shame, which is exactly the prison in which they found themselves. The truth is nothing would ever look the same for them, even God's creation.

As you might imagine, their nakedness was not the issue; the issue was shame! When God opened their eyes to see (know) both good and evil, they saw that they were naked and for the first time, they experienced shame, even though they had been naked ever since creation. They had eaten of the fruit of the forbidden tree and their nakedness now produced shame—intense shame. Had they only chosen to eat from the tree of life, their nakedness would have been "a thing of beauty and a joy forever."

This is a thumbnail of what happened: Sin, taking opportunity through Adam and Eve's new ability to know good and evil, used their holy, righteous, good naked bodies to produce shame. The shame made evident the differences their nakedness revealed.

I might add, with this newfound ability to see and to know good and evil, it was difficult enough for Adam to deal with the shame brought about by having Eve see his nakedness (and vice versa), but you can rest assured that even the thought of God seeing their nakedness brought terror!

What follows? They tried to cover their private parts with fig leaves, of all things! Sound familiar? It should! We have all done it many times. "They sewed fig leaves together and made

---

[5]   Merle A. Fossum and Marilyn J. Mason, *Facing Shame: Families in Recovery* (London: W. W. Norton & Company, 1986), ix.

themselves loin coverings" (Genesis 3:7). How many times have you tried to cover your private parts, the secrets you keep hidden deep within, with some form of fig leaf? The sad truth is this: when we try to hide, we only breed more shame. Secrets always breed shame—always!

At any rate, their shame drove them to hide from each other. Adam could not bear the thought of Eve's seeing his naked body, and neither could Eve bear the thought of Adam's seeing hers!

What they did not understand was this: God had a reason for the No Trespassing sign. He knew there was no way they would obey it, and He also knew (in the big scheme of things) that their inability to obey this No Trespassing sign would be the only thing that would ultimately drive them to tree of life. Of course, their immediate concern was to rid themselves of this terrible shame they were experiencing; however, they were short on thread, and the fig leaves were too small and too thin!

Have you ever noticed that man (and woman) still has a problem being naked in front of others (well, most of us)? How could something that had so perfectly blended into God's creation that it went unnoticed become something so painfully and shamefully obvious? It did because the road to independence from God is filled with potholes of pain and shame.

Interestingly, shame has to do with my perception of who I am, not what I do. When I experience shame, it sends this strong and convincing message to me: you are inadequate, unworthy, useless, inferior, guilty, dumb, stupid, unloved, and unlovely! The moment I believe it, I allow shame to determine my identity. Unfortunately, shame breeds more shame, which serves only to reinforce my perceived identity.

Look at what follows: "And they heard the sound of the Lord God walking in the garden in the cool of the day, and the man and his wife hid themselves from the presence of the Lord God among the trees of the garden" (Genesis 3:8). Now this gets serious! They were no longer simply trying to hide from each other; they were now trying to hide from God! Can you see the scene? Being keenly aware that they have disobeyed God, they heard the very last sounds they want to hear—God's footsteps and God's voice: "Where are you?" (Genesis 3:9). Interestingly, the hide-and-go-seek game did not last long. The Seeker found the hiders very quickly! Actually, He knew exactly where they were, albeit they really did not want Him to find them because they did not want Him to see them in this shameful condition. It really is rather difficult to hide from God. I wonder why we think we can. "And he [Adam] said, 'I heard the sound of Thee in the garden, and I was afraid because I was naked; so I hid myself'" (Genesis 3:10; brackets mine). What a beautiful picture of something that most miss: God, not man, is the seeker—always! "There in none who seeks for God" (Romans 3:11b). In fact, we hope He does not find us. The reason should be obvious.

Juren Beumer, in his biography of the renowned and beloved Henri Nouwen, had this to say about seeking God:

> Monks who live in a monastery as if they have found God are not true monks. I came here to come closer to God, but if I ever let myself believe that I am closer to God than anyone else, I would only be fooling myself. We must search for God, but we cannot find God. We can only be found by Him.[6]

Obviously, the fig leaves were an inadequate covering—very inadequate. God's questions make it evident: "Who told you that you were naked? Have you eaten from the tree of which I commanded you not to eat?" (Genesis 3:11). Now it got very serious! To be sure, no one was laughing—no one but the serpent! I can almost feel Adam's pulse as it races along with his depraved mind to come up

---

6   Jurjen Beumer, *Henri Nouwen: A Restless Seeking for God* (New York: The Crossroad Publishing Company, 1999), 42.

with one final effort to exonerate himself before God. Quickly it comes and it is classic: "The woman whom Thou gavest to be with me, she gave me from the tree, and I ate" (Genesis 3:12).

Oftentimes it is interesting to try to determine what is not said in a passage, and this is one of those times. I think what was not said in this dialogue could have been something like this: *I tried my best to tell You I did not need this woman. You know as well as I that she has been nothing but trouble from the start. Whatever made You think that I needed a helper anyway? I was doing just fine without her! She made me eat that nasty fruit. I told her repeatedly that I did not even like that kind, but she insisted. She finally wore me down to the place where I just gave in and ate the miserable stuff. She caused this whole mess!*

Of course, she had her own defense: "Then the Lord God said to the woman, 'What is this you have done?' And the woman said, 'The serpent deceived me and I ate'" (Genesis 3:13). The truth finally comes out! I might add that this was the first indication of light in this entire dark tragedy. Obviously, when she realized she had been deceived, the deception ended! Although there was nothing she could do to repair the damage done by her disobedience, at least she knew she had been deceived; she knew she had bought the lie—lock, stock, and barrel! The serpent had used that one, holy, righteous, good "Thou shalt not" commandment to deceive her into believing she could live without the benefit of the tree of life. Now, that is deception—exceedingly sinful deception!

Notice this, too: it was God and God alone who brought her out of the darkness of deception! His question was the secret: "What is this you have done?" (Genesis 3:13). I might add this—it is always God and God alone who brings us out of the darkness of deception.

The first Adam, first man fell by making the wrong choice; consequently, his perfect relationship with God was destroyed, and man was left incomplete and on his own!

Questions for Study

1. Was this first Adam, first man really complete?

2. What indicated Adam and Eve made the only free choice man ever made?

3. Explain why question 2 is true.

4. What choice did Adam make?

5. When Adam made the choice to eat of the forbidden tree, what other choice did he make?

6. Other than God, what gave Adam the toughest problem?

7. What was the serpent's purpose in tempting Eve?

8. I indicated that the serpent accomplished his first mission very quickly. What was it?

9. What would prove to be the serpent's long-term course of action?

10. In the serpent's no-holds-barred, all-out mission to deceive Eve, what was his purpose?

11. What was the immediate consequence of Adam's and Eve's eyes being opened?

12. What was their response to seeing their nakedness?

13. I indicated that Adam and Eve tried to cover their private parts with the fig leaves. Apply this to your life.

14. What was God's reason for the "Thou shalt not rule"—the No Trespassing sign?

15. How could something that had so perfectly blended into God's creation that it went unnoticed become something so painfully and shamefully obvious?

16. When you experience shame, what strong and convincing message does it send to you?

17. Why did Adam and Eve try to hide from God?

18. In this hide-and-go-seek game, who was the seeker?

19. How did Adam attempt to exonerate himself before God?

20. What was Eve's defense?

21. What was the first indication of light in this entire dark tragedy?

22. Who led Eve out of the darkness of her deception?

23. What was the consequence of the fall?

4

THE CONSEQUENCES FOR THEIR DISOBEDIENCE

For the Serpent

> And the Lord God said to the serpent, "Because you
> have done this, cursed are you more than all cattle,
> and more than every beast of the field; on your belly
> shall you go, and dust shall you eat all the days of
> your life; and I will put enmity between you and the
> woman, and between your seed and her seed; He shall
> bruise you on your head, and you shall bruise him on
> the heel." (Genesis 3:14–15)

I do not know what the serpent had envisioned about his life, but
whatever it was, it just changed! Think about these consequences:
you are cursed more than any other beast; you will eat dust all the
days of your life; there will be mutual hatred between you and the
woman and between your seed and her seed; and in fact, you will
soon be crushed! I really like the way Paul said it: "And the God
of peace will soon crush Satan under your feet" (Romans 16:20).
Without realizing it, the serpent just lost the battle, even the big

battle; albeit, in time he would be made aware—painfully, aware. So much for the serpent. I do not like giving him attention anyway.

For the Woman

"To the woman He said, 'I will greatly multiply your pain in childbirth, in pain you shall bring forth children; yet your desire shall be for your husband, and he shall rule over you'" (Genesis 3:16).

Again, I do not know what Eve envisioned about her life, but whatever it was, it too just changed! Take a more careful look at the implications of what God said to Eve: For starters, from now on, your husband will rule over you. In addition, I am going to give you a very strong sexual desire for him. Furthermore, you are going to have much pain every time you deliver a baby. In fact, I am going to turn the heat up—high! Moreover, there will be no birth control; in fact, you will be the mother of all the living! "Now the man called his wife's name Eve, because she was the mother of all the living" (Genesis 3:20).

For the Man

> Then to Adam He said, "Because you have listened to the voice of your wife, and have eaten from the tree about which I commanded you, saying, 'You shall not eat from it'; cursed is the ground because of you; in toil you shall eat of it all the days of your life. Both thorns and thistles it shall grow for you; and you shall eat the plants of the field; by the sweat of your face you shall eat bread, till you return to the ground, because from it you were taken; for you are dust, and to dust you shall return." (Genesis 3:17–19)

Obviously, life as Adam had known it in the garden was over—forever over. Before his fall, God handed everything to him on the proverbial silver platter; however, he now had to make it on his own, by the sweat of his brow, only to finish as he had entered—in a handful of dust.

Questions for Study

1. Specifically, what was the *consequence* of Eve's sin? Is that consequence applicable today?

2. Specifically, what was the *consequence* of Adam's sin? Is that consequence applicable today?

3. Is there a difference between the consequences for sin and the punishment for sin?

5

THE PUNISHMENT FOR THEIR DISOBEDIENCE

The truth is the punishment for Adam and Eve's disobedience was much worse than the consequences and far worse than either of them anticipated, even though God had clearly warned them! Listen to what God said to them:

> Then the Lord God said, "Behold, the man has become like one of Us, knowing good and evil; and now, lest he stretch out his hand, and take also from the tree of life, and eat, and live forever"—therefore the Lord sent him out from the garden of Eden, to cultivate the ground from which he was taken. So He drove the man out; and at the east of the garden of Eden He stationed the cherubim, and the flaming sword which turned every direction, to guard the way to the tree of life. (Genesis 3:22–24)

To summarize: God carried out the death sentence, and He did so swiftly—very swiftly! *"THE LORD WILL EXECUTE HIS WORD UPON THE EARTH, THOROUGHLY AND QUICKLY"* (Romans 9:28). Do you not remember what God said? "In the day that you eat from it you shall surely die" (Genesis 2:17). Holiness never compromises, and neither does love; therefore, God removed them from the garden and thereby ended His relationship with them. After all, when they ate the fruit of the forbidden tree, they made the choice not to need Him.

Malcolm Smith, in his book *The Power of the Blood Covenant,* had something very noteworthy to say about this death:

> Man and woman died in the moment they ate of the tree. But what do we mean by death? After all, they continued to live for many years and the human race is still here. Granted, everyone dies in the end; but the warning was that in the day they ate, they would die. The problem with defining death is that those who are in the state of death are doing the defining and are convinced that they are alive! From their perspective, they are alive now and death is what happens at the end of the physical life; but the Bible plainly says that outside of Christ, they are not alive now! This is the world of the walking dead who do not live but exist.[7]

Did you notice that Adam called his wife's name Eve because she was the mother of all the living (Genesis 3:20)? In my opinion, this should have been quite an honor; however, this "mother of all the living" (speaking of humans, of course) was now residing outside the garden, in a much-degraded condition, and unable to return. It was no better for Adam. If Eve was the mother of all the living, surely Adam was the father of all the living—the first man.

This was their real problem: they were dead to God and consequently no longer had access to Him! The flaming sword that turned in every direction, along with the cherubim, relentlessly guarded the gate. Those long, intimate walks with God in the cool

---

7   Malcolm Smith, *The Power of the Blood Covenant* (Tulsa, OK: Harrison House, 2002), 28.

of the evening were to be no more! In the big scheme of things, nothing else mattered. Only one thing really mattered and in their minds. It was this: "How can we reenter the garden and return to that place where life was good?" Sadly, the answer was very clear; they could not reenter the garden! "So He drove the man out; and at the east of the garden of Eden He stationed the cherubim, and the flaming sword which turned every direction, to guard the way to the tree of life" (Genesis 3:24). "For the wages of sin is death" (Romans 6:23a).

Martyn Lloyd-Jones describes the problem this way:

> By nature, then, men and women are under the dominion and the authority and the power of the Devil, who rules this world. He is "the god of this world" (2 Corinthians 4:4). He is "the prince of disobedience" (Ephesians 2:2). So the problem confronting every man and woman in this world is not just a problem of certain sins and weaknesses, nor the desire to get the happiness that they do not have, together with a certain amount of understanding and hope and joy— those are not their problems. The problem confronting every one of us is how to escape from the dominion of Satan, how to get out of the clutches of the Devil, how, somehow, to make an exit out of the kingdom of darkness into the light and knowledge of God, how to get back into that paradise from which we have been thrust, how to get past that flaming sword.[8]

With the flaming sword and the cherubim, God declared that the gate of the garden was forever closed, not just to Adam and Eve but to every person of Adam's race. We simply cannot reenter the

---

8   Martyn Lloyd-Jones, *The Gospel in Genesis: From Fig Leaves to Faith* (Wheaton, IL: Crossway Books, 2009), 84.

garden—period! The members of Adam's race cannot reenter the presence of God. The gatekeepers are relentless protectors.

Can you imagine the shock? One minute Adam was enjoying a perfect love relationship with his wife and with God, and the next minute the whole thing had fallen apart! On the other hand, God was angry—really angry! They did the only thing He told them not to do, and He caught them red-handed. They quickly learned this important lesson about God: escape His wrath, regardless of the cost!

I know we passed by the fig leaves in a hurry, but did you notice what God did just before He sent Adam and Eve out of the garden? In my opinion, this is very important, especially in light of the fact that we are thinking about the punishment for disobedience. Listen to the passage: "And the Lord God made garments of skin for Adam and his wife, and clothed them" (Genesis 3:21). *Honey from the rock!*

This just might be God's first hint of the most wonderful news ever announced. An animal had been sacrificed, blood spilled, and a covering made! Do you think this might possibly mean that where sin increases, grace abounds even more? Now that *would be good news,* but it would probably be too good to be true. Even so, do you think this just might mean that God forgave Adam and Eve? Is it possible that this sacrificed animal, this shed blood, and this covering of skin were a shadow of something *good* to come? Could this be *honey from the rock*? Absolutely. However, take note: shadows only point to the substance; they are not the substance, and therefore, they are not efficacious (effective).

Not one member of Adam's race will ever be able to reenter the garden, eat the fruit of the tree of life, and live forever—regardless of how diligently he or she might try. However, God will show mercy to whom He chooses to show mercy, even if it is Adam and Eve. "He says to Moses, 'I will have mercy on whom I have mercy, and I will have compassion on whom I have compassion'" (Romans 9:15). In spite of how it might seem, this is, indeed, *honey from the rock.*

Unfortunately, we will have to wait until we get home to find out if this first couple made it. However, we do know this: if they made it home, then we can surely say with Paul, "So then it does not depend on the man who wills or the man who runs, but on God who has mercy" (Romans 9:16). If they did not make it home, the same is true. I contend that that is some of the best news ever announced— *honey from the rock*—because it removes the responsibility for my salvation from my shoulders and places it right where it belongs—in God's hands!

Oh well, what can we say? "And the Law came in that the transgressions might increase; but where sin increased, grace abounded all the more, that, as sin reigned in death, even so grace might reign through righteousness to eternal life through Jesus Christ our Lord" (Romans 5:20–21)! *Honey from the rock!*

Contrary to popular opinion, our problem is twofold: Adam and God. On the one hand, we are Adam's offspring (he was the first man, first Adam; see 1 Corinthians 15:45–47) and therefore, we have his sinful, depraved seed in us. On the other hand, we have offended God. When all is said and done, we are helpless and hopeless to solve either of these problems. "Therefore, just as through one man sin entered into the world, and death through sin, and so death spread to all men, because all sinned" (Romans 5:12). "For all have sinned and fall short of the glory of God" (Romans 3:23). Please note that we have come short of the *glory* of God!

Again, contrary to popular opinion: (1) sin is a *not* a transgression of the laws of man or the laws of the church; (2) sin is *not* comprised of a list of symptoms that man has determined are the evidence of sin; and (3) sin is not an illness that produces the aforementioned symptoms. Yes, sin can be defined as a violation of God's law, but it is much more.

Above all things, sin is a very strong power that works in the members of our body, using the holy law of God to deceive us into believing the lie of all lies: that we can, by our obedience, maneuver past the gatekeepers, reenter the garden, eat of the tree of life, and live forever. And I might add, we fall prey to this lie very quickly.

For the record, in my opinion, this is sin's single-most important mission. Ironically, what it does not realize, however, is that in doing this, it is playing right into the hands of the Holy Spirit.

> For sin, taking opportunity through the commandment, deceived me, *and through it killed me.* So then, the Law is holy, and the commandment is holy and righteous and good. Therefore, did that which is good become a cause of death for me? May it never be! Rather it was sin, in order that it might be *shown to be sin by effecting my death through that which is good,* that through the commandment sin might become utterly sinful. (Romans 7:11–13 NASB, emphasis mine)

Honey from the rock!

What is this death that the power of sin brings about as it works in the members of our bodies to deceive us into believing that through our obedience we can get past the gatekeepers and reenter the garden? It is death to our own self-efforts (religious works).

Obviously (and contrary to popular opinion), this death is a perfect example of the fact that God causes all things to work together for good for those who love Him and are called according to His purpose (see Romans 8:28). Satan, working through the power of sin, was convinced that his deception had worked for his good, but he had underestimated the wisdom and power of God.

Before I move on, let me attempt to answer a question you are probably asking. If you were paying attention, you noticed that Paul made it clear that sin, using the holy law of God to bring about our death, demonstrated its exceeding sinfulness. *The question*: How does that show sin as being exceedingly sinful? *The answer*: Sin is so incredibly evil that it would use the holy law of God to deceive us into believing the lie of all lies—that our obedience counts for something, namely a ticket to reenter the garden, eat of the tree of life, and live forever. I might add, we are easy prey for this deception.

With that sidebar, let's return to the message. It is out of this death that life comes—real life! Abundant life! Life in Christ! The "I have been crucified with Christ" life! The "I no longer live; Christ lives in me" life! *Honey from the rock life!* Sin is not happy about that!

Ever since the first couple's expulsion from the garden, man has been trying, *through his own self-effort*, to get past the gatekeepers, back to where life was good, but no one has been able to accomplish that feat, not one. Sacrifices and offerings of all varieties have been offered, but none of them have proven efficacious. The simple truth is this: Adam's race cannot reenter the garden and eat of the tree of life and live forever. God declared it so by placing the flaming sword and the cherubim to guard the entrance to the gate, and as I said earlier, they are relentless gatekeepers.

Furthermore, until God gives faith to someone, that someone is merely seeking the good life, as he or she has no interest in the tree of life (Jesus), and he or she cannot have such an interest. This is a further indication of the severity and gravity of the punishment for sin.

I also want you to notice that God not only permanently expelled Adam and Eve from the garden, but He also sentenced them to a lifetime of hard labor—futilely cultivating the very earth from whence they came. Try as they might, they would never produce a crop or raise an animal that would earn them reentrance into the garden. This should be a warning sign to us, but I am afraid sin has already deceived most churchgoers into believing that lie of lies, and they bought it—hook, line, and sinker.

Take a look at how this played out with Cain and Abel:

> Now the man had relations with his wife, Eve, and she conceived and gave birth to Cain, and she said, "I have gotten a manchild with the help of the Lord." And again, she gave birth to his brother, Abel. And Abel was a keeper of flocks, but Cain was a tiller of

the ground. So it came about in the course of time that Cain brought an offering to the Lord of the fruit of the ground. And Abel, on his part also brought of the firstlings of his flock and of their fat portions. And the Lord had regard for Abel and for his offering; but for Cain and for his offering He had no regard. Then the Lord said to Cain, "Why are you angry? And why has your countenance fallen? If you do well, will not your countenance be lifted up? And if you do not do well, sin is crouching at the door; and its desire is for you, but you must master it." (Genesis 4:1–7 NASB)

Yes, the Lord did have regard for Abel and for his offering (a shadow; a sign), but that regard did nothing to cause the gatekeepers to relent and thereby give him access back into the garden. As for Cain, the Lord completely rejected him and his offering. If you will read the next several verses, you will find that he left the presence of the Lord and lived in the land of Nod as a vagrant and a wanderer. The fact is neither of them could master sin. It is simply too powerful for anyone to master. You can rest assured that sin deceived both Cain and Abel into believing their offerings would prove efficacious. Their parents certainly hoped so! Please note that Abel's offering required the shedding of blood, which was indeed a sign of what was to come, but unfortunately, the blood of bulls and goats isn't sufficient to distract the gatekeepers, not even for a second. And I might repeat, signs are just that—signs.

Contrary to popular opinion, on the one hand, God was very selective in choosing His family members, in choosing His Son's Bride; on the other hand, He wasn't so selective in choosing who among us would be Adam's family members, as every one of us was included—no exceptions.

To be sure, not one of those of us He chose to be in His family deserve to be there, not to mention that God's standard for membership into His family is very, very high—too high for any of us to reach! Why, then, did He choose some and reject others? I can only tell you what the scriptures tell us: "So then He has mercy on whom He desires, and He hardens whom He desires" (Romans 9:18). *Honey from the rock!*

With that, let us look forward, way down the road, and see what we can find about this predicament in which humanity finds itself: "Therefore, just as through one man sin entered into the world, and death through sin, and so death spread to all men, because all sinned" (Romans 5:12). Surely, each of us can identify with this one man! Of course, he was Adam, the same Adam we have been discussing! Did you notice, however, that *all sinned*—every one of us? Did you notice that death spread to all men—every one of us? This means you and me (just a reminder)!

It gets even clearer: "Nevertheless death reigned from Adam until Moses, even over those who had not sinned in the likeness of the offense of Adam, who is a type of Him who was to come" (Romans 5:14). In other words, nobody escapes death, not even those who had not sinned the way Adam did when he chose to eat the fruit of the tree of knowledge of good and evil! You see, from Adam until Moses, there was no law—no No Trespassing signs. Man was on his own, doing his own thing, satisfying his desire to be independent, and showing God just how smart he really was.

Now listen carefully: "So then as through one transgression there resulted condemnation to all men ... For as through the one man's disobedience the many were made sinners" (Romans 5:18a–19a). Do you get the picture? Because Adam chose to eat from the tree of knowledge of good and evil, each of his offspring (that includes you and me) is a dead-to-God -sinner, terribly offensive to Him, eternally separated from Him, destined and doomed to hell, and completely helpless and hopeless to do anything about it. Sadly, we deserve a lot worse!

In my opinion, James Montgomery Boice's comments in his commentary on Romans 5–8 are very helpful. This is what he had to say:

First, Paul explained the sense in which "all sinned." He did not mean that all have become sinners and have therefore sinned, though we would naturally think this, but rather that each of us was declared a sinner because of Adam's original sin or transgression. It is true that we also sin and should be condemned for that, if there were nothing more to be said. But that is not Paul's meaning. He meant that all have been accounted sinners in Adam, so that those who were going to be saved could be accounted righteous in the Lord Jesus Christ.[9]

Face it! You came out of your mom's womb "born in Adam" and in the aforementioned sinful condition! Yes, I know that everyone thought you were sweet and cute; in fact, most were certain you would be the next Billy Graham or Mother Teresa! Your grandmother probably thought that you were a little angel! Even so, let me tell you what God thought:

There is none righteous, not even one; there is none who understands, there is none who seeks for God; all have turned aside, together they have become useless; there is none who does good, there is not even one. Their throat is an open grave, with their tongues they keep deceiving, the poison of asps is under their lips; whose mouth is full of cursing and bitterness; their feet are swift to shed blood, destruction and misery are in their paths, and the path of peace have they not known. There is no fear of god before their eyes. (Romans 3:10–18)

---

[9] James Montgomery Boice, *Romans; Volume 2: The Reign of Grace; Romans 5–8* (Grand Rapids, MI: Baker Book House, 1992), 6020.

Do you get it? Paul is talking about us—you and me—and he is correct, which means our mom was wrong, our grandmother was wrong, and so were all the rest of those so deceived!

I could go on, but let me summarize: because you and I are the offspring of Adam, we were born with his depraved, sinful seed in us. Furthermore, because Adam sinned, we were born sinners—dead to God! We arrived on the scene having absolutely no inclination toward Him—none at all. We were not only offensive to Him, but He was also very offensive to us. The tree with the No Trespassing sign nailed to its trunk looks just as good to us as it did to Adam and Eve! Remember: "For the wages of sin is death" (Romans 6:23a).

I will give you this word of encouragement: He does have some inclination toward some of us, and He describes that inclination by this wonderful and beautiful word—*grace* (a.k.a., one-way love)! *Honey from the rock!*

Are you ready for some good news—very good news? Here it is: *the tree of life came to us*, and when He came, He came in "hot pursuit" of us.

> Arise my darling, my beautiful one, and come along. For behold, the winter is past, the rain is over and gone. The flowers have already appeared in the land; the time has arrived for pruning the vines, and the voice of the turtledove has been heard in our land. The fig tree has ripened it figs, and the vines in blossom have given forth their fragrance. Arise, my darling, my beautiful one, and come along! O my dove, in the clefts of the rock, in the secret place of the step pathway, let me see your form, let me hear your voice; for your voice is sweet, and your form is lovely. (Song of Songs 2:10–14 NASB)

You might disagree, but that sounds like "hot pursuit" to me. Oh, and by the way, this Pursuer always catches those He pursues—every one of them. "Of those whom Thou hast given Me I lost not one" (John 18:9b). It was, indeed, grace that moved Him to send the tree of life to us! *Honey from the rock!*

Tullian Tchividjian, in his book *One Way Love: Inexhaustible Grace for an Exhausted World*, gives the most succinct and accurate definitions of grace I had ever read: "Grace is unconditional acceptance given to an undeserving person by an unobligated giver. It is one-way love."[10] In other words, grace is one-way love that has nothing to do with us and all to do with Him. What that says, among other things, is this: Jesus is well aware of our condition, so He doesn't require or expect anything from us. He knows we are completely helpless to get past the gatekeepers. All He asks is that we allow Him to love us. Because He came to you, you can cease trying to get past the gatekeepers and rest in Him and in His finished work!

> For by grace have you been saved through faith; and that not of yourselves, it is the gift of God; not as a result of works, that no one should boast. For we are His workmanship, created in Christ Jesus for good works, which God prepared beforehand, that we should walk in them. (Ephesians 2:8–10 NASB)

Honey from the rock!

Maybe it is time for you to cease striving to get past the gatekeepers, to die to your own self-efforts, and discover the "I no longer live; I have been crucified with Christ" life; "the life I now live, I live by faith in the Son of God, who gave Himself up for me" life.

---

[10] Tullian Tchividjian, *One Way Love: Inexhaustible Grace for an Exhausted World* (David C. Cook Distribution Canada, 2013) p. 33.

Questions for Study

1. God punished the serpent in a very specific way. What was it?

2. God punished Eve in a very particular way. What was it?

3. God punished Adam in a very particular way. What was it?

4. What did God do to prevent Adam and Eve from reentering the garden and eating of the tree of life and thus, living forever?

5. What is God using to prevent those of us who were born in Adam—Adam's ancestors—from reentering the garden and eating of the tree of life and thus, living forever?

6. What did God do concerning the fig leaves, just before He sent Adam and Eve out of the garden?

7. What might be the significance of these garments of skin?

8. Humanity's problem was twofold. Explain.

9. What is God's standard for membership into His redeemed, justified, perfect family?

10. How did Abel manage to meet God's standard of perfection? Or did he?

11. What seems to be the only common denominator of those who have gained membership into God's family?

12. How did sin enter into the world and thereby defile everyone?

13. What about the condition of those who lived between Moses and the law and therefore, who did not sin in the way Adam sinned?

14. Since man cannot get past the gatekeepers and reenter the garden, what did God do that enables His elect to eat of the tree of life?

6

TWO FAMILIES: ADAM'S
AND GOD'S

As I trust you now see, we came into this world hopelessly lost, sinfully depraved, separated from God, and on our way to hell. Fortunately, however, none of this changed the love of God or the holiness of God. In spite of our having been born in Adam and our resulting depravity, He continues to be the same loving and holy God He has always been, even toward us. This becomes obvious as we realize the significance of His having chosen to do for some of us that which none of us could have done for ourselves—redeem us and bring us home.

Hopefully, it has become evident by now that each of us was born into the family of the first Adam, first man, and as a result, what was true about him became true about us. I also trust that you now realize we were hopeless to do anything about our family predicament. Fortunately, however, God has always been intent on redeeming some of us from this terrible fall. Isaiah called them a remnant. "And Isaiah cries out concerning Israel, 'Though the number of the sons of Israel is as the sand of the sea, it is the remnant that will be saved …'" (Romans 9:27). *Honey from the rock!*

Just how did He accomplish this? Well, step one (though He did not accomplish it in steps) was to begin a new family—a family with absolutely no relationship to the first Adam, first man, a family entirely free from Adam's seed—God's perfect, holy family, whose Head would be the last Adam, second man.

> So also it is written, the first man, Adam, became a living soul. The last Adam became a life-giving spirit. However, the spiritual is not first, but the natural; then the spiritual. The first man is from the earth, earthy; the second man is from heaven. (1 Corinthians 15:45–47)

As you remember, God created Adam from the dust of the earth and breathed into him the breath of life; however, God did not create Jesus, the last Adam, second man, from the dust of the earth. In fact, Jesus was conceived by the Holy Spirit as the result of the imperishable seed of the Word of God entering the virgin womb of Mary. Jesus (last Adam, second man) was born, therefore, of God's seed and consequently, free from the seed of Adam. God identified Jesus as the second man because he is the man (human) God designated to be the head of the second significant family—His chosen family. God identified Jesus as the last Adam because there would never be the need for another Adam. *Honey from the rock!*

Before I move on, there are two other things I want you to know about this last Adam, second man.

(1) He existed long before the first Adam, first-man ever thought about existing! I realize that sounds a bit strange, but it is nevertheless very true. You see, He is eternal, which means He has no beginning nor ending. "Thou, Lord, in the beginning didst lay the foundation of the earth, and the heavens are the works of Thy hands; they will perish, but thou remainest; and they all will become old as a garment, and as a mantle Thou wilt roll them up, as a garment they will also be changed. But Thou art the same, and Thy years will not come to an end" (Hebrews 1:10–12). "Jesus Christ is the same yesterday and today, yes and forever" (Hebrews 13:8).

45

(2) He was born of a woman and born under the law. "But when the fullness of the time came, God sent forth His Son, born of a woman, born under the Law, in order that He might redeem those who were under the Law, that we might receive the adoption as sons" (Galatians 3:4–5). That means that He was born a Jew—a true Jew—and that is significant!

Paul had this to say regarding a true Jew: "For he is not a Jew who is one outwardly; neither is circumcision that which is outward in the flesh. But he is a Jew who is one inwardly; and circumcision is that which is of the heart, by the Spirit, not by the letter; and his praise is not from men, but from God" (Romans 2:28–29).

Paul also had this to say about Gentiles being grafted into the true vine and thus, becoming true Jews. "You will say to me then, 'Branches were broken off so that I might be grafted in.' Quite right, they were broken off for their unbelief, but you stand by your faith" (Romans 11:19–20a). "For if you were cut off from what is by nature a wild olive tree, and were grafted contrary to nature into a cultivated olive tree, how much more shall these who are the natural branches be grafted into their own olive tree?" (Romans 11:24).

Fortunately, the traits of God's family are significantly different from those of Adam's family! Every member of God's family is born, as was Jesus, free from Adam's seed—a saint, not a sinner; a pleasure to God, not offensive to Him; in perfect relationship with Him, not in a broken relationship with Him; having hope, not hopeless; freed from sin, not enslaved to sin; enslaved to righteousness, free from unrighteousness; destined for heaven, not doomed to hell; free from the guilt of sin, not condemned; free from the penalty of sin, not facing the wages of sin—to mention a few.

One would think all people would be keenly interested in finding out just how they might leave Adam's sinful, depraved family and enter into God's redeemed, righteous family; however, this is not the case. If you have been around for any time at all, you know that is not the case. The gospel is offensive—very offensive—so much so that only the Holy Spirit can make it attractive! If you do not believe this, go back and revisit the Jews' response to it. Why, the scribes and Pharisees labeled Jesus as a blasphemer! "And the scribes and the Pharisees began to reason saying, 'Who is this man who speaks blasphemies? Who can forgive sins, but God alone?'" (Luke 5:21).

As I told you earlier, God is very fussy about who becomes a part of His family. In fact, His requirement for membership is perfection, and not only perfection but perfection according to *His* idea of perfection! "Therefore you are to be perfect, as your heavenly Father is perfect" (Matthew 5:48). Furthermore, He shows mercy on whom He chooses to show mercy and He hardens who He chooses to harden, regardless of how perfect we might see ourselves. "So then He has mercy on whom He desires, and He hardens whom He desires" (Romans 9:18). *Honey from the rock!*

Loraine Boettner, in his book *The Reformed Doctrine of Predestination*, has this to say:

> The Reformed Faith has held to the existence of an eternal, divine decree which, antecedently to any difference or desert in men themselves separates the human race into two portions and ordains one to everlasting life and the other to everlasting death. So far as this decree relates to men, it designates the counsel of God concerning those who had a supremely favorable chance in Adam to earn salvation, but who lost that chance. As a result of the fall they are guilty and corrupted; their motives are wrong and they cannot work out their own salvation They have forfeited all claim upon God's mercy, and might justly have been

> left to suffer the penalty of their disobedience as all
> of the fallen angels were left. But instead the elect
> members of this race are rescued from this state of guilt
> and sin and are brought into a state of blessedness and
> holiness. The non-elect are simply left in their previous
> state of ruin, and are condemned for their sins. They
> suffer no unmerited punishment, for God is dealing
> with them not merely as men but as sinners.[11]

From all indications, Abel, Adam's firstborn, was one of the first ones to whom He chose to show mercy, though not enough mercy to allow him to return to the garden. However, I must admit that I cannot wait to see what happened to his dad and mom! Most of us would probably be very upset if we learned that *they* made it into heaven and especially so if we found out that some of our good, churchgoing, Bible-totin' friends did not.

I know you can explain why we would be angry, but just in case you cannot, I will do it for you. We think we are more deserving than Adam and Eve; after all, none of us has ever done anything nearly as sinful as their sin (or so we think!). Hold on before you react to that and remember this: there was nothing in any of us, even you and me, to cause Him to desire us—nothing! He just picked some of us after the counsel of His own will and for His own glory. "Also we have obtained an inheritance, having been predestined according to His purpose who works all things *after the counsel of His will*, to the end that we who were the first to hope in Christ should be to the praise of His glory" (Ephesians 1:11–12, emphasis mine). *Honey from the rock!*

I do have some more good news: If you have any inclination for Jesus, then you are one of God's elect, one of those He foreknew, predestined, conformed to the image of His Son, called, justified, and

---

11 Loraine Boettner, *The Reformed Doctrine of Predestination* (Phillipsburg, NJ: Presbyterian and Reformed Publishing Company, 1932), 83.

glorified! Now, that is good news—*honey from the rock*! Furthermore, if you have any inclination for Jesus, you are probably already asking this question: How can I leave Adam's family and enter into God's family? Well, the truth is, if you have an inclination for Jesus, He has already delivered you from the kingdom of darkness—Adam's sinful, depraved family—and transferred you to the kingdom of His dear Son—God's family! My dear friend, you are already home— truly home. *Honey from the rock!* Even so, I think it might be a bit beneficial to consider some of the personal dynamics of this incredible miracle.

First, you would do well to realize that you did not leave Adam's family on your own, and neither did you enter God's family on your own. The tree of life came to you! You did not go to Him; in fact, you could not and you did not desire to do so. You simply cannot save yourself! Make no mistake! This miracle of redemption is the work of the triune Godhead—the Father, the Son, and the Holy Spirit! Honey from the rock! God initiates the work and the Holy Spirit brings it to pass through the finished work Jesus accomplished in your behalf on the cross. You see, if God had not initiated this miracle, it would have never happened because you could not have initiated it. You were dead to God! Remember? To be sure, without the work of the Holy Spirit, you would have never been drawn to Jesus because your had no inclination for Him. Finally, apart from the finished work of Jesus, there is no new family, no redemption, and no eternal life.

Second, it would behoove you to realize that this miracle is a matter of grace (i.e., you cannot and do not and will not deserve it—period). When God chose to deliver you from Adam's depraved, sinful family and to transfer you to His redeemed, righteous family, it was a thing of incredible grace, not to mention, mercy. "For He delivered us from the dominion of darkness, and transferred us to the kingdom of His beloved Son, in whom we have redemption, the forgiveness of sins" (Colossians 1:13–14). *Honey from the rock!* In doing so, He made two choices: (1) He chose not to give you what you deserved (mercy), and (2) He chose to give you what you did not deserve (grace). The moment you decide to add anything to His grace, you are acting as if you can earn His righteousness. All works-based righteousness is self-righteousness, and God hates self-righteousness!

Third, and finally, it would be very beneficial if you would accept the fact that this new life is a life of faith—relentless trust in the finished work of Jesus. After God initiates the miracle by placing His seed into your life, He then gives you the faith to believe His seed has accomplished His purpose in your life. You see, saving faith is not something you "will" into existence, and neither is it something you conjure in your mind; instead, it is God's incredibly gracious gift to you. By the way, God saves you so you can believe, not the other way around. *Honey from the rock!*

What, then, is the evidence God has given you this gift of faith? It is this and only this: your inclination for Jesus—nothing more, nothing less. Do not allow your emotions to dictate the reality of this faith; instead, receive and embrace that inclination. And whatever you do, do not allow the Enemy to deceive you into believing the evidence God has given you this faith is somehow related to your behavior! A pig is a pig not because he oinks, squeals, or eats slop but because he was born a pig! If God has given you saving faith, then His seed is in you, and you are born of God. The evidence has nothing to do with your behavior and all to-do with His lavished grace. *Honey from the rock!*

I think Paul summed it up quite well with this:

> For by grace you have been saved through faith; and that not of yourselves, it is the gift of God; not as a result of works, that no one should boast. For we are His workmanship, created in Christ Jesus for good works, which God prepared beforehand, that we should walk in them. (Ephesians 2:8–10)

Honey from the rock!

This is what Dr. D. Martyn Lloyd-Jones, who at the time was pastor of Westminster Chapel in London, had to say in his commentary of Ephesians 2:

> Now then it all comes to this: You notice that he starts with the word "For"—"For grace ye are saved." It is a continuation; he is looking back to what he has been saying, and then he puts it all once more in a manner that we should never forget. This is a description of what it really means to be a Christian. More and more am I convinced that most of our troubles in the Christian life really arise at that point. For if we are not right at the beginning we shall be wrong everywhere.[12]

If you are reading this but have no inclination for Jesus, I can only pray He will place His seed into your life and thereby initiate in you what He has initiated in so many others—a genuine desire for Jesus. To be honest, I doubt you would be reading this if you had no inclination for Him.

Having made my case for salvation by grace alone through faith alone in Jesus alone, I now want to remind you of Jesus's exchange with Nicodemus, a ruler of the Jews:

> Nicodemus: "Rabbi, we know that You have come from God as a teacher; for not one can do these signs that You do unless God is with him."

> Jesus: "Truly, truly, I say to you, unless one is born again, he cannot see the kingdom of God."

---

[12] D. Martyn Lloyd-Jones, *God's Way of Reconciliation: Studies in Ephesians Chapter 2* (Grand Rapids: Baker Book House, 1972), p.129.

Nicodemus: "How can a man be born when he is old? He cannot enter a second time into his mother's womb and be born, can he?"

Jesus: "Truly, truly, I say to you, unless one is born of water and the Spirit, he cannot enter into the kingdom of God. That which is born of the flesh is flesh, and that which is born of the Spirit is spirit. Do not marvel that I said to you, 'You must be born again.' The wind blows where it wishes and you hear the sound of it, but do not know where it comes from and where it is going; so is everyone who is born of the Spirit.'"

Nicodemus: "How can these things be?" (John 3:1–9)

From this passage, it is obvious Jesus was emphatically telling Nicodemus he must be born again if he expected to see the kingdom of God; consequently, we must not take His admonition lightly. The fact is we must be born again because there is no other way out of Adam's family—none whatsoever.

Notice the question Nicodemus raised with Jesus: "How can a man be born when he is old?" That's a good question if you ask me! Notice also that Jesus did not answer his question; instead, He compared those so born with the wind. I get the impression that Jesus did not want Nicodemus to get the mistaken idea that he (Nicodemus) could somehow facilitate the experience.

Although Jesus left the answer to Nicodemus's question pretty much up in the air, Paul gives us much insight in Romans 6. Let us have a look:

Or do you not know that all of us who have been baptized into Christ Jesus have been baptized into His death? Therefore, we have been buried with Him through baptism into death, in order that as Christ

was raised from the dead through the glory of the
Father, so we too might walk in newness of life. For
if we have become united with Him in the likeness of
His death, certainly we shall be also in the likeness of
His resurrection, knowing this, that our old self was
crucified with Him, that our body of sin might be done
away with, that we should no longer be slaves to sin;
for he who has died is freed from sin. (Romans 6:3–6)

In my opinion, this is scripture's clearest picture of what Jesus
meant when He said, "Except a man be born again, he cannot see
the kingdom of God."

In this text, Paul makes it very clear that the Holy Spirit has
baptized every believer into Christ Jesus—a done deal. Every
believer is in Christ, and His seed is therefore in us, firmly implanted
and bearing the intentioned, predestined fruit. "For we are His
workmanship, created in Christ Jesus for good works, which God
prepared beforehand, that we should walk in them" (Ephesians
2:10). Having established that, let us now examine some of the
specifics that are involved.

Because the Holy Spirit has baptized us into Christ Jesus, He
has by definition baptized us into Jesus's death. In other words, we
cannot have one without the other. That old Adamic man (our old
self) was so offensive to God that a second chance for him was out
of the question. God had no choice but to kill him, to destroy him,
to do away with him, to eliminate him. Because God is love, holy,
and just, He could never receive that depraved, sinful Adamic man
into His perfect and holy family.

How and when did the death of this Adamic man take place?
This Adamic man was crucified in Christ. Listen to these words of
the Paul: "I have been crucified with Christ" (Galatians 2:20a). As
a believer, you can reckon this true: when Jesus was crucified on
the cross, the old, Adamic man was crucified in Him! He is dead—
graveyard dead!

Now notice Paul's progression: "Therefore we have been buried with Him through baptism into death" (Romans 6:4a). Can you see it? Paul wants us not only to know that that Adamic man is dead, but he also wants us to know he is buried! In other words, we no longer have to deal with him. This is an incredibly important piece of information, especially in light of the fact that so many Christians believe they must, on a daily basis, attempt to kill that old man. What a difference this makes in the life of the believer! *Honey from the rock!*

As we now see, that old Adamic man has been crucified and buried; however, there is more—much more. You see, if this were the end of the story, the story would have a very sad ending because God's family would be nonexistent.

Let us continue to follow Paul's progression: "In order that as Christ was raised from the dead through the glory of the Father, so we too might walk in newness of life. For if we have become united with Him in the likeness of His death, certainly we shall be also in the likeness of His resurrection" (Romans 6:4b–5). Can you see this? A new creation has just arrived on the scene of life—a new creation in Christ Jesus. This new creation is new because he has been born of the seed of God—holy, righteous, and accepted in the beloved! Good news indeed! *Honey from the rock!*

Let me summarize: That old, sinful Adamic man is crucified, dead, and buried; he no longer exists. Furthermore, God has miraculously given birth to a new creation, a creation in which His seed abides. We can now say that old Adamic man died and was born again by the imperishable seed of the Word of God, a new creation in Christ Jesus. This new creation no longer has Adam's seed abiding in him! He is a new creation, with God's imperishable seed abiding in him—a new member of God's family. "Do not marvel that I said to you, 'You must be born again'" (John 3:7). "For you have been born again not of seed which is perishable but imperishable, that is, through the living and abiding word of God" (1 Peter 1:23).

I want us to continue to follow Paul's progression in this sixth chapter of Romans and discover the benefits of having been born again; however, I first want to remind you that although we have discussed how God dealt with that sinful, Adamic man, we have yet to discuss just how God dealt with our sins. That discussion will be forthcoming.

Back to Romans 6 and the benefits of our having been released from Adam's family and born again by the seed of God into His redeemed family:.

1. We walk in newness of life (v. 4).
2. Our bodies of sin have been done away with (v. 6).
3. We are no longer slaves to sin (vv. 6–7, 14, 18, 20, 22).
4. We are free from sin because we are dead to sin (vv. 7, 11).
5. We are alive to God (v. 11).
6. We are no longer under the law's jurisdiction (v. 14).
7. We live under grace (v. 14).
8. We are slaves of righteousness (v. 18).
9. We are sanctified (v. 22).
10. We have eternal life (vv. 22–23).

In my mind, this is good news—*honey from the rock!* If you think about it, old things have passed away and new things have come! *Are you in Adam, or are you in Christ?*

Questions for Study

1. How did we enter into this world?

2. How did the way we entered into the world affect God's love for us?

3. Into which family were you physically born—Adam's family or God's family?

4. I indicated that God has always been intent on redeeming some of us from the terrible fall—delivering us from Adam's family and transferring us to God's family. What text verifies this?

5. Who did God set in place as the head of His family?

6. What ties did this last Adam, second man have with the first Adam, first man?

7. As you remember, God created Adam from the dust of the earth and breathed into him the breath of life. How did God arrange for Jesus's entrance on the earth?

8. Why did God identify Jesus as the last Adam, second man?

9. I indicated that there were two significant things one should remember about this last Adam, second man. What were they?

10. Why are these things significant?

11. Do the scriptures indicate that the Gentiles will be able to enter God's family?

12. How are the traits of God's family different from the traits of Adam's family?

13. One would think all people would be keenly interested in finding out just how they might leave Adam's sinful, depraved family and enter into God's redeemed, righteous family; however, this is not the case. Why?

14. Who was one of the first to whom God gave membership into His family?

15. How does God determine who He will allow into His family?

16. If you have an inclination for Jesus, I indicated you were probably already asking this question: How can I leave Adam's family and enter God's family? How can you?

17. List three of the personal dynamics of the incredible miracle of being delivered from the kingdom of darkness and transferred to the kingdom of God's dear Son—that is, being delivered from Adam's family and transferred to the family of God.

18. What was Jesus's response to Nicodemus's question, "How can a man be born when he is old?"

19. Jesus clearly said to Nicodemus, "Unless one is born again he cannot see the kingdom of God"; therefore, we must take this seriously. Let me ask the logical question: How is one born again?

20. What is the significance of your having been baptized into Jesus's death?

21. What is the significance of your having been buried with Jesus?

22. What is the significance of your having been united with Christ in the likeness of His resurrection?

23. What are some of the benefits of your having been released from Adam's family and born again with the seed of God, into God's redeemed family?

24. Are you in Adam, or are you in Christ?

7

GOD'S TREATMENT OF OUR SINS

Just for the record, I have written a booklet entitled *God's Treatment of Sin: Perfect and Permanent,* which deals with this subject in much more detail than in this brief treatise. But for now, let me raise this question: What really happened on the cross? The usual and pat answer goes something like this: Jesus died for my sins so I can go to heaven when I die. Although this is correct, it falls short of the whole truth. Actually, there are two sides to this proverbial coin: (1) how God dealt with the sinful, Adamic man, and (2) how God dealt with our sins.

As I showed in the last section, God crucified that old Adamic man in Christ on the cross. Thankfully, he is nonexistent. In this section, however, I want us to see just how God dealt with our sins through Jesus's vicarious sacrifice.

Imagine for a minute a list of every sin you will have committed during your entire lifetime. If you live only seventy years and commit only one sin per day, your list will contain almost twenty-six thousand sins! If perchance you commit two sins per day, then your list will contain almost fifty-two thousand sins! Now be honest and imagine your list. (Your need for a savior might just be much greater than you thought!)

Thankfully, Peter tells us that Jesus bore our sins in His body on the cross so that we might die to sin and live to righteousness: "And

He Himself bore our sins in His body on the cross, that we might die to sin and live to righteousness, for by His wounds you were healed" (1 Peter 2:24). This is what Paul said to Titus: "Who gave Himself for us that He might redeem us from every lawless deed and purify for Himself a people for His own possession, zealous for good works" (Titus 1:14–15). *Honey from the rock!*

Now I want you to use your imagination again and place every sin that is on your list (your certificate of debt) into the body of Jesus as He hangs on the cross. Now, let me ask you again, what happened on the cross? Can you see it? In bearing your sins in His body on the cross, Jesus also bore the guilt of your sins! "He made Him who knew no sin to be sin on our behalf" (2 Corinthians 5:21a). God declared Jesus guilty of your sins! *Honey from the rock!* Give this time to settle into your thinking.

Because we know that God is holy, loving, just, and righteous, what is the next step in this progression? God must punish Jesus for the sins He is bearing in His body on the cross—yours and mine! Get this straight: God killed Jesus, separating Himself from Jesus, thereby extracting from Him the wages of sin, wages that we should have paid. *God punished Jesus for your sins,* and He did so to the full extent of the law's requirement! Now listen carefully to His words: "My God, My God, why hast Thou forsaken Me?" (Matthew 27:46).

If your imagination is still working, you are keenly aware that because Jesus bore your sins in His body on the cross, He also bore the guilt of your sins; consequently, God punished Him for your sins— past, present, and future. Now for the most incredibly good news you will ever hear—well, almost: Jesus became your scapegoat and took your sins away, so far away that God will never remember them again! *"For I will be merciful to their iniquities, and I will remember their sins no more" (Hebrews 9:12). "And their sins and their lawless deeds I will remember no more" (Hebrews 10:17). Honey from the rock!*

Now for the grand finale—well, almost: as the result of Jesus's vicarious suffering and death, God has forgiven you—forever forgiven you for everything! You are past, present, and future forgiven! You get off scot-free! *Honey from the rock!* There is no sweeter word in the English language than the word *forgiven*, especially to one who is guilty and knows he is.

In the end, what does this mean for this new creation, you who are in Christ Jesus? It means God has imputed His righteousness to you. To say that another way, as an act of extreme mercy, Jesus has taken ownership of your sinful record, and as an act of lavish grace, He has given you ownership of His perfect, spotless record! God no longer charges your sins against you because He has already charged them against Jesus!

> Now all these things are from God, who reconciled us to Himself through Christ, and gave us the ministry of reconciliation, namely, that God was in Christ reconciling the world to Himself, *not counting their trespasses against them*, and He has committed to us the word of reconciliation. (2 Corinthians 5:18–19, emphasis mine)

> And when you were dead in your transgressions and the uncircumcision of your flesh, He made you alive together with Him, *having forgiven us all our transgressions, having canceled out the certificate of debt* consisting of decrees against us and which was hostile to us; and He has taken it out of the way, having nailed it to the cross. (Colossians 2:13–14, emphasis mine)

> *Honey from the rock!*

This new creation is now the righteousness of God in Christ—justified, sanctified, and glorified!

> He made Him who knew no sin to be sin on our behalf, that we might become the righteousness of God in Him. (2 Corinthians 5:21).

But God being rich in mercy, because of His great love with which He loved us, even when we were dead in our transgressions, made us alive together with Christ (by grace you have been saved), and raised us up with Him, and seated us with Him in the heavenly places, in Christ Jesus, in order that in the ages to come He might show the surpassing riches of His grace in kindness toward us in Christ Jesus. (Ephesians 2:4–7)

Honey from the rock!

I think Malcolm Smith does a good job of summarizing this:

God the Son would take to Himself our humanity, live out our human life, suffer and die as us, and shed the blood of God. Only then could sin be remembered no more. A blood had to be shed that transcended human blood as the Creator transcends the creature. Jesus, the God-Man, appointed to be the High Priest of the new covenant, laid aside the glory that belonged to Him as the Son of God and came among us as a carpenter in Nazareth. He was both the High Priest and the sacrifice. On the cross He, as Priest, offered Himself as the final sacrifice that all sacrifices since the first blood shed in Eden had pointed to. It is not a wonder that in Eden the man and the woman actually desired the death of God so that they might take His place, but in pursuing this desire they died. God responded to their rebellion with infinite love; He placed Himself in the hands of the creature human and died with the result that the human is made alive, is forgiven and reconciled.[13]

---

[13] Malcolm Smith, *The Power of the Blood Covenant* (Harrison House; Tulsa, OK, 2002) p. 112.

Now that this new creation is the righteousness of God in Christ, God has some incredibly good news for you.

> Since therefore brethren, we have confidence to enter the holy place by the blood of Jesus, by a new and living way which He inaugurated for us through the veil, that is, His flesh, and since we have a great priest over the house of God, let us draw near with a sincere heart in full assurance of faith, having our hearts sprinkled clean form an evil conscience and our bodies washed with pure water. (Hebrews 10:19–22)

For the first time, you can enter the holy place, and you can do so with a sincere heart—boldly—because of Jesus's finished work! *Honey from the rock!* The veil of separation has been rent in twain from the top to the bottom (meaning He did it), thereby giving you access to Him! Now, do the obvious and *draw near to Him*! By the way, religion (self-righteous works) is the seamstress that is trying to repair the veil that Jesus tore in two.

Wait! He has more for you—much more:

> But God, being rich in mercy, because of His great love with which He loved us, even when we were dead in our transgressions, made us alive together with Christ (by grace you have been saved), and raised us up with Him, and seated us with Him in the heavenly places, in Christ Jesus, in order that in the ages to come He might show the surpassing riches of His grace in kindness toward us in Christ Jesus. For by grace you have been saved through faith; and that not of yourselves, it is the gift of God; not as a result of works, that no one should boast. (Ephesians 2:4–9).

Can you see it? God has not only imputed His righteousness to you, thereby giving you access to Him, but He has also raised you up with Jesus and seated you in the most holy place, at His right hand! Thus, the finished work of Jesus, and that, my dear friend, is good news—*honey from the rock!*

Just for a moment, I want to make a practical application. Use your imagination again and imagine that tomorrow you, this new creation, will commit adultery. Surely, we both know that God has defined adultery as sin, so we cannot escape the fact that you will have committed an act God has defined as sin.

In light of all I have said thus far, I raise this question: Now that this new creation has committed adultery, what must you do for God to restore you to right relationship with Him? Yes, I do know the usual and pat answer: you must confess, repent, and ask God for His forgiveness. If that answer is correct, then you no longer need Jesus to be your righteousness because confessing, repenting, and asking for forgiveness have become your means to righteousness.

The truth is there is nothing you can do, and neither is there anything you need to do because: (1) Jesus has already done everything that will ever be necessary to maintain your righteousness; and (2) committing adultery did *not* cause you to lose your relationship with God, not even your fellowship with Him, because Jesus has already borne your sins in His body on the cross, become guilty of them, been punished for them, taken them away, and forgiven you— forever forgiven you! "And the Law came in that the transgression might increase; but where sin increased, grace abounded all the more, that, as sin reigned in death, even so grace might reign through righteousness to eternal life through Jesus Christ our Lord" (Romans 5:20–21). *Honey from the rock!*

For those of you who are jumping ahead with the obvious question, I will raise it: Does this mean that we should sin even more, so that grace might abound? To use the words of Paul: "May it never be! How shall we who died to sin still live in it?" (Romans 6:2). Obviously, we cannot continue to practice sin because God's seed abides in us; in fact, we cannot sin because we have been born of God. "No one who is born of God practices sin, because His seed abides in him; *and he cannot sin*, because he is born of God" (1 John 3:9, emphasis mine). *Honey from the rock!*

What it does mean is this: you will commit every sin for which Jesus died on your behalf (conservatively, all fifty-two thousand–plus of them); however, you cannot commit a sin for which Jesus has not already paid the penalty in full. In other words, you cannot out-sin the grace of God. What you will notice as you begin to embrace this truth is: (1) your heart yearns to please the one who did such a remarkable thing in your behalf, and (2) you are walking through this life with an ever-increasing heart of thanksgiving. You can count of this!

The late Robert Farrar Capon, Episcopal priest and author, in his book *The Mystery of Christ*, does a magnificent job of expressing what I am purposing to communicate, using the example of homosexuality.

> Enough of this moral wrangling though: each of us has paid his ethical money and made his moral choice. All we can reasonably do on the level of the scholastic morality game is either respect each other's choice (even if we don't agree with it), or try to argue each other out of the positions we've so far bought. But for as long as we insist on playing such a game, that's the best we can expect. So let me quit the sport of abstract ethics and get back to my objection to even discussing the "sinfulness" of homosexuality or anything else. From a biblical and theological point of view, that whole approach to the human condition begs two very important questions. First, it assumes that sinning is simply a conscious, voluntary bit of business that we could avoid if only we would make the effort—if only we would just obey the Law of God, and thus render ourselves sinless. And second, it assumes that such self-acquired sinlessness has been stipulated by God

as the essential precondition of His favor toward us. Both of those assumptions, however, are dead wrong not only theologically but scripturally. To see the error in the first one, go back and read Romans 7: that's the chapter in which Paul most clearly insists that sin is an indwelling condition we can't get rid of by any effort of our own, and which even the Law of God, in all its holiness, righteousness, and goodness, only aggravates. We are, he says, "sold under sin"—helpless slaves of it, not the masters of our fate that scholastic ethics implies we are. And to see the error in the second assumption, take a look at Romans 5:8: that's where Paul says that God "proves His love for us in that while we were still sinners Christ died for us"— thus scotching once and for all the notion that God has made sinlessness on our part a condition of His grace. So the theological upshot of all this is pretty much a draw. If homosexual acts are sinful, you're still not allowed to run around pretending that God can't or won't forgive homosexual persons unless they abstain from such acts; and if they're not sinful, but still repugnant to you, you're not allowed by common decency to make your tastes the standard for other people's behavior. Either way, your first duty is to love such people as they are and not to imply that God has given you permission to hold an axe over their heads. Because if God has really done what the Epistle to the Romans says He has, He's gone ahead and solved all His problems with sin independently of what sinners might or might not do about it. [14]

---

[14] Robert Farrar Capon, *The Mystery of Christ: and Why We Don't Get It* (Grand Rapids, MI: William B. Eerdmans Publishing Company, 1993), 51–52.

Back to the idea of confessing, repenting, and asking God for His forgiveness. I do not want to leave you thinking these have no place in the life of this "new creation you" because they do, indeed; however, probably not as you think. Confessing is by definition agreeing with God, and certainly, we want to do just that; however, to confess sins for which Jesus has already paid the penalty is to disagree with God. Furthermore, to repent of sins for which Jesus has already paid the penalty is also to disagree with God. Finally, asking God for His forgiveness for sins for which Jesus has already paid the penalty is, again, to disagree with God. So let us see if we can agree with Him rather than disagree with Him.

To agree with Him, we must see confession as agreeing with God about our believing a lie—namely, that this sin has broken my relationship or my fellowship with God. Furthermore, we must see repentance as our turning from the lie and embracing the truth, the truth that I have not lost my relationship or fellowship with God as the result of my committing adultery. Finally, we must see forgiveness not as something for which we must ask or beg but as something that is already ours.

Please allow me to share something from my life that I trust will illustrate what I am saying. In September of 1960, I began my college journey at Asbury College in Wilmore, Kentucky. Just before my parents and I left for the trip from my hometown of Reynolds, Georgia, to Wilmore, Daddy came into my room and handed me several blank checks from the business checkbook and said very matter-of-factly, "Use these to pay for your expenses at Asbury." I had already been privileged to sign the business checks to pay the bills for the business. As you might imagine, I was very familiar with the work it took to keep the business in the black, so his directive made me very nervous.

The day soon came for me to write a check to Asbury for fall tuition, which, at the time, seemed like more money than God had, at least to me. I will never forget what I did. When I saw the how much money was due, I got out of the line and called Daddy, asking him what I was to do, as the amount was quite large. I will also never forget his response: "Mac, I told you to use those checks for your expenses." He actually seemed to be a bit perturbed I had called with that question. I wrote the check, but not without much anxiety and guilt. Not long after that experience, I had to buy the books for the quarter. I wrote the check, but I did not sleep a wink that night out of concern that he might not have enough money in the bank to cover so much money in one day. I kept that up all quarter. Every time I had to write a check, I did so with anxiety and guilt, even fear. I made it through those first four years of college, and he insisted that I follow that plan the entire way. By the way, I still have some of those checks!

In case you missed it, my point is this: Daddy gave me everything I needed to pay for my college career. All I had to do was receive his gracious gift. He never expected me to apologize for spending the money (though I did so quite frequently!), and neither did he expect me to repay him, not one red cent (thought I felt terribly guilty about not doing so), and he certainly never expected me to beg him to provide the money. Had I attempted to do any of these things, I would have insulted his graciousness. I had to become a father to understand what he had done. Two things became very clear to me: (1) Daddy loved me without condition; (2) he trusted me with his hard-earned money; and (3) he loved me more than he loved money—much more.

I tell you all of that so I can tell you this: your heavenly Father has given you everything you need for life and godliness (2 Peter 1:3), and He expects nothing in return. You do not have to beg Him for what He has already given to you. Nothing thrills your Father's heart like His watching you freely receiving His gracious gifts. Hopefully you have realized that you already have everything you are striving to gain.

With that, let me summarize: (1) God took the initiative to begin a new, perfect family and to place Jesus at its head; (2) God took the initiative to crucify our Adamic man; (3) God took the initiative to bury that Adamic man; (4) God took the initiative to raise a new creation in Christ Jesus; (5) God took the initiative to place His perfect, imperishable seed in this new creation; (6) God declared that in Christ we have met His standard for membership into His perfect, redeemed family; and (7) God took the initiative to invite you draw near to Him and to sit at His right hand in Jesus.

You see, it really is *all* about Him; we are merely benefactors of His finished work!

Questions for Study

1. What is the usual and pat answer to this question: What happened at the cross?

2. There are two sides to the proverbial coin concerning what happened at the cross. What are they?

3. Jesus made five significant accomplishments concerning our sins through His vicarious death on the cross. What are they?

4. What role does each of the following play in the life of a Christian: confession, repentance, and asking for forgiveness?

5. Explain how God's treatment of our sin was all about God's doing, not ours

8

THE COVENANT OF LAW

In this section, I want to share some thoughts with you about the unfortunate state most people live in for many years after they come into the family of God—the state of religious performance. As I told you earlier, this is precisely the state I lived in for many of the early years of my Christian life. In the end (or the beginning, for that matter), it is attempting to gain God's acceptance and love by keeping the Ten Commandments, along with all the interpretations of those commandments that are imposed upon us by certain significant others in our lives (a.k.a., performance-based acceptance).

Right out of the chute, I want to tell you that Christianity is *not* a religion—not by any stretch of the imagination! Christianity is an intimate love relationship with Jesus that thrills the heart of God. Even so, many of those who call themselves Christians are fully persuaded that their performance is a vital part of this relationship. They somehow believe the success of the relationship depends upon Jesus and them, not upon Jesus alone—religion dressed to the nines.

To explain this, I must introduce two concepts I have not heretofore mentioned: the old covenant and the new covenant. I think Malcolm Smith does an excellent job of contrasting these two covenants:

> The old covenant is the covenant that was made with Israel at Mount Sinai through Moses, their

representative. It was the covenant of the law of the Ten Commandments, the sacrificial system of offering up lambs, bulls, and goats to cover the sins of the people; the mark and seal of membership in the covenant was the circumcision of the male. The new covenant is called new because it made all that went before it old and of no more use as a means of salvation. It was not just another covenant that improved on the previous one, as this year's automobile model is an improvement over last year's. The word "new" means new in kind, that which has never been thought or dreamed of before. This covenant is mediated by the Lord Jesus and established in His blood. Membership is in being sealed by the Spirit of God, who writes the law on the heart and in the desires of men and women. He is the power of the covenant enabling those within it to live it promises.[15]

As I am sure you know, God is a God of covenant. The pages of the Bible make this evident, as it tells of the various covenants He made with men, such as Noah and Abraham. Of course, the most famous of God's covenants is the one He made with the Israelites after He had set them free from Egyptian slavery—the covenant of law. God's promise in this covenant was this: "Now then, if you will obey My voice and keep My covenant, then you shall be My own possession among all the peoples, for all the earth is Mine; and you shall be to Me a kingdom of priests and a holy nation" (Exodus 19:5–6). As strange as it might seem, the Israelites promised to do everything the Lord required! "And all the people answered together and said, 'All that the Lord has spoken we will do!' And Moses brought back the words of the people to the Lord" (Exodus 19:8).

---

[15] Ibid., 12.

As you can see, the success of this covenant of law depended not upon God but upon the obedience of the Israelites, and strangely, they thought they could hold up their end of the bargain. Talk about deception!

Just for the record, let me remind you of the law they promised to keep—the Ten Commandment (Exodus 20:1–17): (1) You shall have no other gods before Me. (2) You shall not make for yourself an idol or any likeness of what is in the heaven above or on the earth beneath or in the water under the earth. (3) You shall not take the name of the Lord your God in vain. (4) Remember the Sabbath day to keep it holy. (5) Honor your father and your mother. (6) You shall not murder. (7) You shall not commit adultery. (8) You shall not steal. (9) You shall not bear false witness against your neighbor. (10) You shall not covet. Amazingly, they promised to obey—perfectly!

For the people to obey God's commandments, they had to be interpreted. As you can imagine, this proved to be quite a challenge, especially when it came to agreement regarding the interpretation. Look, for example, at the first one: you shall have no other gods before me. I wonder how many committee meetings it took to determine just who these "other gods" were. Then there is the second commandment: you shall not make for yourself an idol or any likeness of what is in the heaven above or on the earth beneath or in the water under the earth. Can you imagine how many laws it took just to carry out this one law? At any rate, by the time they had finished their interpretation, they had more pages than the IRS tax code does today; well, not quite, but almost. It is my understanding that there were 210 laws that had to do with keeping the Sabbath day holy!

My point is this: in their sincere effort to keep the Ten Commandments, they had to add even more laws to be certain they were following every jot and tittle. As you can imagine, they were on a futile mission. In spite of their very best efforts, they would fail to keep their part of the bargain. Interestingly, God knew this from the beginning, but they insisted. "By works of the Law no flesh will be justified in His sight; for through the Law comes the knowledge of sin" (Romans 3:20). *Honey from the rock!*

Think back with me to the garden experience: When Adam and Eve chose to eat the fruit of the tree of knowledge of good and evil, they chose to live their lives under the false assumption that they could not only discern good and evil but also perform the good and avoid the evil. After years and years of Adam's family trying to follow this plan, God intervened and in essence said this: Obviously, I was right in the beginning; your way is the way of death. However, I am going to give you one more opportunity. I am going to give you the rules. I am going to define for you in very simple terms what you have been trying to discern—good and evil. I will detail for you what you must do and what you must avoid doing to gain My acceptance, and I will do so in ten words—ten commandments. Obviously, when you were on your own, you could not discern good and evil, much less perform the good or avoid the evil, so let us see how you will do when I spell out good and evil for you. And God gave Moses the Ten Commandments.

As you know, the Israelites did no better at keeping the Ten Commandments than they did at discerning good and evil. Interestingly, God was not surprised; however, man has continued to insist that he can do his part and thereby impress God. I think we easily forget that God's standard is perfection; consequently, almost is not good enough! In other words, eight out of ten gets a failing grade, even nine out of ten! The truth is even ten out of ten gets a failing grade because righteousness does not come through the law—period. "If a law had been given which was able to impart life, then righteousness would indeed have been based on law" (Galatians 3:21b).

Because of man's continued and futile effort to obtain righteousness by following the Ten Commandments, he has unwittingly made them objects of worship. Unfortunately, they have become one of the "other gods" that God, with the first commandment, warned us not to worship. The number of modern-day churches that post the

Ten Commandments in conspicuous places, thereby informing the worshipper that obeying them is his means to right standing with God, evidences this. Sadly, the tree of knowledge of good and evil continues to be more appealing than the tree of life.

Unfortunately, the church all too often sends the same message to modern-day worshippers that God sent to Israel in the old covenant of law—if you obey God's voice and keep His commandments, He will bless you with acceptance, love, and value, even eternal life. This is religion, pure and undefiled, and its end is death!

It is time now for me to make something very clear: God never intended for the law to be our means to righteousness! Much to the contrary, He gave us the law for the following five reasons.

1. To give us knowledge of sin—"Because by works of the Law no flesh will be justified in His sight; for through the Law comes the knowledge of sin" (Romans 3:20).
2. To define sin—"On the contrary, I would not have come to know sin except through the Law; for I would not have known about coveting if the Law had not said, 'YOU SHALL NOT COVET'" (Romans 7:7).
3. To show us the exceeding sinfulness of sin—"But sin, taking opportunity through the commandment, produced in me coveting of every kind; for apart from the Law sin is dead" (Romans 7:8).
4. To give sin its power—"For apart from the Law, sin is dead" (Romans 7:8b). "The sting of death is sin, and the power of sin is the law" (1 Corinthians 15:56).
5. To be a child trainer (tutor) to lead (drive) us to Jesus—"Therefore the Law has become our tutor to lead us to Christ, that we may be justified by faith" (Galatians 3:24).

To be sure, the old covenant was a covenant of law, not a covenant of righteousness. It was a covenant between God and the Israelites, and its success depended upon their obedience to the law—the Ten Commandments, along with all the interpretations of them. Unfortunately, they could not hold up their end of the bargain. Of course, admitting this was impossible, so for centuries and centuries they have continued in this futile effort to gain acceptance (righteousness) with God, and in doing so, they have rejected the tree of life—Jesus!

Although I am well aware that most Christians, like all Jews, hold the Ten Commandments in a place of very high esteem, I want to show you how the new covenant (Testament) Scriptures identify them.

1. The law of sin and death—"For the law of the Spirit of life in Christ Jesus has set you free from *the law of sin and death*" (Romans 8:2, emphasis mine).
2. The ministry of death—"But if *the ministry of death*, in letters engraved on stones, came with glory, so that the sons of Israel could not look intently at the face of Moses because of the glory of his face, fading as it was, how much more shall the ministry of the Spirit fail to be even more with glory" (2 Corinthians 3:7, emphasis mine)?
3. The ministry of condemnation—"For if *the ministry of condemnation* has glory, much more does the ministry of righteousness abound in glory" (2 Corinthians 3:9, emphasis mine).

In my opinion, this is evidence, par excellence, that Adam and Eve made a tragic mistake when they rejected the tree of life! Look back at the previous verses and see the contrasts.

1. The law of sin and death versus the law of the Spirit of life in Christ Jesus.
2. The ministry of death versus the ministry of the Spirit.
3. The ministry of condemnation versus the ministry of righteousness.

In these contrasts, we have a bird's-eye view of some of the advantages of the new covenant of grace over the old covenant of law. They should be obvious, but just for the record: the old covenant is a covenant of sin and condemnation, a ministry of death, whereas, the new covenant is a covenant of righteousness and life in Christ Jesus, a ministry of the Spirit. In my opinion, these differences are worthy of note, especially if you are one of those who have made the Ten Commandments an object of your worship.

At this point, I want to make it clear that—even though God never intended the law to make us righteous and even though the scriptures do identify the law as the "law of sin and death," "the ministry of death," and the "ministry of condemnation"—*the law is holy, righteous, and good*. Listen to the words of Paul: "So then, the Law is holy, and the commandment is holy and righteous and good" (Romans 7:12). How can this be, in light of the aforementioned truths?

The law is holy, righteous, and good because: (1) God is its author; (2) it is an expression of God's character—His holiness; (3) it gives us knowledge of sin; (4) it defines sin for us; (5) it shows us the exceeding sinfulness of sin; (6) it gives sin its power; and therefore, (7) it is a child trainer that leads (drives) us to Jesus.

In other words, the law of Moses does have a good, holy, righteous purpose; namely, to drive us in hopeless despair to Jesus, who is our righteousness. It accomplishes this by showing us our inability to meet God's standard of perfect obedience through our futile efforts at obeying it. *Honey from the rock!*

Hopefully the law has done it work in your life and you are now living in the new covenant, enjoying intimacy with the lover of your soul.

Questions for Study

1. What does the phrase *performance-based acceptance* mean?

2. Define Christianity.

3. Which is the most famous of God's covenants?

4. What was God's promise in this covenant He made with the Israelites?

5. Upon whose shoulders did the success of the covenant of law rest?

6. What was the law the Israelites promised to obey?

7. List the Ten Commandments.

8. What was the result of Israel's effort to interpret the Ten Commandments?

9. What is God's standard for obedience?

10. What is the evidence that many have made the Ten Commandments objects of worship?

11. Did God intend the law to be our means to righteousness?

12. The scriptures enumerate five reasons as to why God gave the law. What are they?

13. How does Paul describe the Ten Commandments?

14. Give a brief contrast between the covenant of law and the covenant of grace.

15. Why does Paul identify the law as being holy, righteous, and good?

9

THE COVENANT OF GRACE

Please pay careful attention to these words:

> But now He has obtained a more excellent ministry,
> by as much as He is also the mediator of a better
> covenant, which has been enacted on better promises.
> For if the first covenant had been faultless, there
> would have been no occasion sought for a second.
> For finding fault with them, He says, "Behold, days
> are coming," says the Lord, "when I will effect a new
> covenant with the house of Israel and with the house
> of Judah; not like the covenant which I made with
> their fathers on the day when I took them by the
> hand to lead them out of the land of Egypt; for they
> did not continue in my covenant, and I did not care
> for them," says the Lord. "For this is the covenant
> that I will make with the house of Israel after those
> days," says the Lord: "I will put My laws into their
> minds, and I will write them upon their hearts. And
> I will be their God, and they shall be My people. And
> they shall not teach everyone his fellow citizen, and
> everyone his brother, saying, 'Know the Lord,' for
> all shall know Me, from the least to the greatest of

> them. For I will be merciful to their iniquities, and
> I will remember their sins no more." When He said,
> "new covenant" He has made the first obsolete. But
> whatever is becoming obsolete and growing old is
> ready to disappear. (Hebrews 8:6–13)

You should note that the author of Hebrews is actually quoting from Jeremiah 31:31–34, where God originally promised this new covenant.

Thus we have the covenant of grace, a better covenant indeed! *Honey from the rock! Very sweet honey!* Michael Horton tells us very succinctly why it is a new and better covenant: "It is a new and better covenant, with Christ himself rather than Moses as its mediator."[16] Even a casual glance will tell you that this new covenant is a better covenant with better promises; in fact, unlike the old covenant between God and man, this is a covenant made between God and Jesus on our behalf. In other words, the success of the covenant depends upon Jesus, not upon us, and that is a very good thing! This covenant actually accomplishes everything that would have been accomplished had Adam and Eve chosen to eat of the tree of life!

Now notice what the writer said in the final two sentences in the above passage: the first covenant—the covenant of law—is obsolete and ready to disappear! I wonder if the Christians of today will ever embrace as truth that the old covenant has grown old, has become obsolete, and is ready to disappear. Incredible! In the next few paragraphs, I want to summarize some of the specific advantages of the new covenant.

In the first place, God wrote His old covenant laws—the Ten Commandments—onto tablets of stone. As you can see, they were "carved into stone" and therefore could offer no grace to the worshipper; however, God wrote His new covenant laws—love God and love one another (the law of the Spirit of life in Christ

---

[16]   Michael Horton, *A Better Way: Rediscovering the Drama of God-Centered Worship* (Grand Rapids: Baker Books, 2002), p.27.

Jesus)—upon the hearts and minds of believers, obviously providing room for much grace. *Honey from the rock!*

You see, the laws God carved onto the tablets of stone have always been arduous—difficult, hard, laborious, grueling, and demanding. However, the laws God wrote upon our hearts have never been arduous; instead, they are easy and light. "Take My yoke upon you, and learn from Me, for I am gentle and humble in heart; and you shall find rest for your souls. For My yoke is easy, and My load is light" (Matthew 11:29–30). *Honey from the rock!*

In the second place, the old covenant was a covenant of works and therefore a covenant of mistrust, whereas the new covenant is a covenant of faith and therefore a covenant of trust. The fact is, when one has to earn what one gets, the element of mistrust is always involved. Questions such as, "Will he pay me fairly and justly?" or "Will he withhold part of my earned wages?" always arise. However, when what one receives is a thing of grace, faith and trust are always present. It is quite incredible to know you will not receive what you deserve but something much better—always! *Honey from the rock!*

In the third place, the old covenant required that the law be kept perfectly but never supplied the power to do so; however, in the new covenant, God has released us from the tyranny of the law. "But now we have been released from the Law, having died to that by which we were bound, so that we serve in newness of the Spirit and not in oldness of the letter" (Romans 7:6). Notice what Paul is telling us in this verse. On one hand, we died to the law and are thereby released from it. On the other hand, we now live in newness of the Spirit, not in oldness of the letter of the law. Again, this is a major advantage for Christian believers because it allows them to live by the leadership of the Holy Spirit rather than by attempting to obey a system of rules they simply cannot obey. The law stirs up disobedience whereas the Spirit stirs up obedience.

In the fourth and final place, the old covenant of law always leaves its worshippers with a consciousness of sin, which, by the way, is the evidence that it does not make its worshippers perfect. However, through the new covenant of grace, Jesus removes our consciousness of sin and thereby evidences the efficacy of His vicarious sacrifice.

> For the Law, since it has only a shadow of the good things to come and not the very form of things, can never by the same sacrifices year by year, which they offer continually, make perfect those who draw near. Otherwise, would they not have ceased to be offered, because the worshipers, having once been cleansed, would *no longer have had consciousness of sins?* But in those sacrifices there is a reminder of sins year by year. It is impossible for the blood of bulls and goats to take away sins. (Hebrews 10:1–4, emphasis mine)

Yes, I know the killing of bulls and goats is foreign to most modern-day Christians (although we make many other sacrifices!); however, to the Jew it was everyday affair. Sadly, the countless daily sacrifices that the priests made on their behalf served only to leave them with a strong consciousness of their own sin. One can only imagine how they longed for God to release them from that terrible, guilt-ridden weight.

Thankfully, the once-for-all sacrifice Jesus made in our behalf worked perfectly. In the end, it removed our sins and therefore our sin consciousness. *Honey from the rock!* The fact that we no longer have a sin consciousness is the evidence His sacrifice worked; albeit, the modern-day Pharisees believe, that for one to claim not to be sin-consciousness is to be self-righteous. I am amazed that so many refuse to give Jesus the credit He deserves for having done what we could have never done for ourselves.

This brief illustration will hopefully clarify my point. A friend of mine was going along in life and doing quite well (or so he thought) when out of nowhere, a small tumor showed its ugly face. He did what most of us would have done. He made an appointment to see his physician. When the physician examined the tumor, he said something similar to this: "This is nothing for you to worry about;

come back in a few days and I will remove it, just for safety's sake." In a few days, he returned to have it removed without incident. The physician did what any physician who is worth his salt would have done; he sent the biopsy to the laboratory for pathological examination, expecting nothing of significance. *However,* when the physician received the report, much to his surprise, the biopsy proved the tumor to be a very rare and malicious, malignant tumor.

As you might imagine, up to this point in my friend's life, he had never given much thought about cancer, and certainly not to his having cancer. However, at precisely the moment he received this tragic news, he became cancer conscious—very cancer conscious.

His physician told him to return to his office because he needed to do a radical excision of the tissue surrounding the tumor, which he did soon thereafter. The physician told him that he felt sure that he got all of the malignant cells and things should be fine, thereby giving my friend a short-lived reprieve from his cancer consciousness. However, he then told him that he believed it was necessary for him to have radiation and chemotherapy, again, just for safety's sake. Of course, upon hearing those words, he immediately returned to his state of cancer consciousness.

As he neared the end of the treatment, the level of his cancer consciousness increased dramatically. Finally, the day came for the final report concerning the treatment and the news was good—very good. The physician told him that the therapy had worked because there were no signs of cancer cells. Again, as you can imagine, the relief was tremendous; no more cancer consciousness! Then the terribly frightening words came from the physician: "I want you to return in three months for a CT scan so we can be certain that the cancer has not returned." Immediately cancer consciousness flooded his mind like a mighty river, and for three months, he battled to think positively when all the while, he could not rid himself of this dreaded cancer consciousness. At the end of the three months, the report was good—very good—and for a brief moment, the cancer consciousness subsided. However, those old, familiar, dreaded words came from the mouth of his physician: "Return in three months for another CT scan so we can be certain the cancer has not returned." Immediately the cancer consciousness returned! In the end, the cancer killed him.

Can you see the similarities between the way the sin-conscious Jews lived and the way my cancer-conscious friend lived? My friend, if Jesus did no more than this through His vicarious sacrifice, then He really did not accomplish anymore than the goats and bulls of the Jewish Day of Atonement.

Listen! When Jesus gave His life for our sins, He took them away, so far away that they will never return—never, ever! He separated them from Himself as far as the east is from the west, never to remember them again! No more CT scans, and no more sin consciousness! *Honey from the rock!*

This, my dear friend, is the heart and essence of new covenant living. Are you a believer who is continuing to purpose to live under the old covenant of law, or are you purposing to rest in Jesus's finished work? You would do well to carefully consider your answer!

Take a few minutes to consider the following comparative chart.

old covenant ... written on tablets of stone
new covenant ... written on our hearts and minds

old covenant ... a covenant of mistrust (work to earn)
new covenant ... a covenant of trust (faith)

old covenant ... produces death
new covenant ... produces life

old covenant ... stirs up disobedience
new covenant ... stirs up obedience

old covenant ... the law of sin and death
new covenant ... the law of the Spirit of Life in Jesus

old covenant ... leaves a consciousness of sin
new covenant ... removes the consciousness of sin

old covenant ... cut with the blood of bulls and goats
new covenant ... cut with the blood of Jesus

old covenant ... cannot take away sins
new covenant ... takes sin away

old covenant ... a shadow of the new covenant
new covenant ... the substance that produced the shadow

old covenant ... required the keeping of the law
new covenant ... releases us from the law

old covenant ... a covenant of works
new covenant ... a covenant of rest

Questions for Study

1. Why is the new covenant, the covenant of grace, a new and better covenant?

2. What are the specific benefits of the covenant of grace?

3. The heart and essence of new covenant living is _____?

4. Is it really possible to live without being sin conscious?

10

⤸⤸⤷⤷

HIS FINISHED WORK

One of the many things that has intrigued me for years is that most Christian believers have a difficult time accepting that this new life in Jesus is not a life of works but a life of rest. For some reason, many believers simply cannot accept that Jesus did a perfect work and sat down, not because He was tired but because He was *finished*. On the cross, He made this quite clear. "It is finished" (John 19:30)! Even so, it is obvious that most Christian believers are determined not to waste a minute of precious time assisting Jesus in His continued effort to redeem mankind. I saw a bumper sticker several years ago that said what I think is in the minds of most: "Look busy; Jesus is coming soon!"

If you are one who is trying to help Jesus finish His work, I have some good news for you—very good news: the work *is* finished, and Jesus has called *you* to a Sabbath *rest!*

> For indeed we have had good news preached to us, just as they also; but the word they heard did not profit them, because it was not united by faith in those who heard. For we who have believed enter that *rest*, just as He has said, "As I swore in My wrath, they shall not enter My *rest*," although His works were finished from the foundation of the world. For

He has thus said somewhere concerning the seventh day, "And God *rested* on the seventh day from all His works"; and again in this passage, "They shall not enter My *rest*." Since therefore it remains for some to enter it, and those who formerly had good news preached to them failed to enter because of disobedience (unbelief), He again fixes a certain day, "Today," saying through David after so long a time just as has been said before, "Today if you hear His voice, do not harden your hearts." For if Joshua had given them *rest*, He would not have spoken of another day after that. There remains therefore a Sabbath rest for the people of God. (Hebrews 4:2–9, emphasis and parentheses mine)

Honey from the rock!

If my count is correct, the word *rest* is used no less than twelve times in chapters three and four of Hebrews. Look for yourself!

As I swore in My wrath, they shall not enter My *rest*. (3:11)

And to whom did He swear that they should not enter His *rest*, but to those who were disobedient. (3:18)

Therefore, let us fear lest, while a promise remains of entering His *rest*, any one of you should seem to have come short of it. (4:1)

For we who have believed enter that *rest*, just as He has said, "AS I SWORE IN MY WRATH, THEY SHALL NOT ENTER MY REST," although His works were finished from the foundation of the world. (4:3)

For He has thus said somewhere concerning the seventh day, "AND GOD *RESTED* ON THE SEVENTH DAY FROM ALL HIS WORKS"; and again in this passage, "THEY SHALL NOT ENTER MY *REST.*" (4:4–5)

For if Joshua had given them *rest,* He would not have spoken of another day after that. (4:8).

There remains therefore a Sabbath *rest* for the people of God. (4:9)

For the one who has entered His *rest* has himself also *rested* from his works, as God did from His. (4:10)

Let us therefore be diligent to enter that *rest,* lest anyone fall through following the same example of disobedience. (4:11)

Notice the unnoticed: failing to enter that rest is disobedience.

John MacArthur, in his commentary on Hebrews, has this to say:

The English "rest" and the Greek word that it translates have similar meanings. The basic idea is that of ceasing from work or from any kind of action. You stop doing what you are doing. Action, labor, or exertion is over. Applied to God's rest, it means no more self-effort as far as salvation is concerned. It means the end of trying to please God by our feeble, fleshly works. God's perfect rest is a rest in free grace.[17]

---

17   John F. MacArthur, *The MacArthur New Testament Commentary: Hebrews* (Chicago: The Moody Bible Institute of Chicago, 1983), 96.

Whatever else we might conclude from these chapters, it should be obvious that the author is attempting to make the people of God aware of that all-important rest God has provided for them through the work He accomplished in Jesus from before the foundation of the world.

Unfortunately, many churchgoers view this rest as an addendum to the finished work of Jesus; consequently, they see it as a work they must accomplish to continue as Christians rather than an actual rest from that work. "The one who has entered His rest has himself also rested from his works, as God did from His" (Hebrews 4:10). Notice the unnoticeable again: "rested from *his* works, as God did from His."

As a result, many use several of the verses from these chapters as evidence to support the heretical view that, if Christians are not diligent in their work, they can lose their fellowship with God, even their salvation. For example, "Take care, brethren, lest there should be in any one of you an evil, unbelieving heart, in falling away from the living God" (Hebrews 3:12). Another example is seen in the next verse: "But encourage one another day after day, as long as it is still called 'Today,' lest any one of you be hardened by the deceitfulness of sin" (Hebrews 3:13).

Obviously, if we are to consider this rest as an essential addition to the finished work of Jesus concerning salvation (justification, sanctification, and glorification), we might well use these verses to develop a fair case for the possibility of a Christian, having been hardened by the deceitfulness of sin, losing his or her salvation. The truth, however, is this: this rest is not an addendum to the finished work of Jesus concerning justification, and neither is it something man must achieve to complete the work Jesus accomplished on the cross. God saves someone by grace alone through faith alone because of Jesus alone, which is the *only* way He saves. No addendum is needed. All that remains for the people of God is this Sabbath rest He has provided for us in Jesus. *Honey from the rock!*

Obviously, there is nothing we *must* do, and neither is there anything we *can* do, to complete His *finished* work. Even the thought is absurd! His work would not be finished were it not complete.

This rest is *not* something we must accomplish! It is the lifestyle God has provided in Jesus for every believer, every saint! It is the fruit of His *finished* work, not the fruit of our *continued* works. It is an eternal rest from the fear of losing the most precious gift anyone could ever receive—eternal life. Furthermore, it is an eternal rest from pretending to be someone you are not, from striving to reach an unreachable goal, from our futile attempts at making ourselves acceptable to the God who said, "Therefore you are to be perfect, as your heavenly Father is perfect" (Matthew 5:48). It is an eternal rest in our Sabbath, who is Jesus. It is God's gift to His elect! *Honey from the rock!*

Unfortunately, because of the deceitfulness of sin, most Christians never *experience* this rest, and the few who do, do so for only brief periods. All too soon, they find themselves back in that familiar struggle to become what God has already declared them to be—saints; consequently, they seldom experience the joy and peace and assurance that true Christianity offers. They become tired, weary, grumpy, angry, and frustrated in their struggle. At best, they live the lives of modern-day Pharisees.

Obviously, the author of the letter to the Hebrews is *not* indicating that one can enjoy being saved today and then lose one's salvation tomorrow! Even to hint of such would eliminate any hope of rest because there is no work like the work we do when we have that mind-set! This author (maybe Paul) is attempting to make us aware that there really is a rest from that very work.

In addition, he is also warning us of the possibility of entering into this rest only to have sin lure us back into that terrible place of legalism. My dear friend, do not be deceived; there really is a Sabbath rest that remains for the people of God! "Let us therefore be diligent to enter that rest, lest anyone fall through following the same example of disobedience" (Hebrews 4:11).

This is the author's warning to those of us who are Christians: "Therefore, let us fear lest, while a promise remains of entering His rest, any one of you should seem to have come short of it" (Hebrews

3:1). In other words, if you are going to be afraid, be afraid that you will come short of this rest! Whatever you do, do not become hardened by the deceitfulness of sin and find yourself striving to become who you already are—a saint, righteous and holy before God. Be diligent to enter this rest!

Do not be deceived! Although Christian believers can fall short of this rest, we can *never* be in danger of losing our salvation! To believe one can lose one's salvation is the ultimate deception for a true Christian. The eternal life God has given to us can never become anything less than eternal! The imperishable seed of the Word of God, from which every one of us is born, can never die. Jesus made it quite clear that those to whom He has given eternal life will never perish.

> My sheep hear My voice, and I know them, and they follow Me; and I give eternal life to them, *and they shall never perish*; and no one shall snatch them out of My hand. My Father, who has given them to Me, is greater than all; and no one is able to snatch them out of the Father's hand. I and the Father are one. (John 10:27–30, emphasis mine)

To be sure, no one works as diligently as the one who believes he can lose his salvation and/or his fellowship with God.

Let me be quick to say this: Christian believers can certainly live far beneath the rest God has provided for us in Jesus! Christians, like the Israelites of old, can wander in the desert of self-centeredness for a long, long time. The truth is many believers have lived and died without consciously entering into the Sabbath rest God has provided for them in Jesus. In a sense, the Israelites of old did the same thing! An entire generation lived and died without entering into Canaan— the land flowing with milk and honey!

Now do not get confused! Every Christian actually lives every moment of every day in the Sabbath rest because Jesus is the Sabbath rest and we live in Him every moment of every day. There is, however, a vast difference between living in that rest without knowing it (falling short of it) and living in that rest and knowing it (consciously entering into it)!

Although Satan is well aware that he *cannot* snatch any of us out of the Father's hand, he is also just as aware that he *can* rob us of the joy and peace and assurance that are rightly ours. He does this by using sin to deceive us into believing this rest is something we must achieve for Jesus's finished work to be complete and to guarantee our justification. It does not take long, however, for us to realize we cannot achieve this rest, though we quickly move into denial. Even so, the harder we work toward achieving it, the more effectively it evades us. Once Satan's scheme is accomplished, we begin to live in "that certain terrifying expectation of judgment and the fury of a fire" (Hebrews 10:27), which is about as far from the Sabbath rest as one can get.

Unfortunately, many Christians believe they see the deceitfulness of sin when sin lures them into some justification for committing an act of sin. For example, let us suppose you are being tempted to steal a coat from a department store, and during the temptation, sin comes and successfully lures you into some justification for stealing the coat. For most Christians, therein is the deceitfulness of sin. I am sure you realize it, but this is exactly what Satan achieved with Adam and Eve in the garden! Every Christian knows and knows well that sin can never be justified.

What happens is this: When we commit an act that God has declared to be sin, we do so because we have justified committing the sinful act. We know that the act of sin is wrong, but we justify doing it. Our thinking is usually something like this: my neighbor stole my lawn mower; therefore, his actions justify my stealing his pressure washer.

Now please pay attention! What I have just described is not, I repeat *not*, the deceitfulness of sin; rather, it is the selfishness of man.

What, then, is the deceitfulness of sin? When sin convinces you that your continued righteousness, your sanctification, depends upon your behavior, it has demonstrated its deceitfulness. To say that another way, when sin convinces you that *you can achieve* the rest that God has provided for you through the finished work of Jesus, it has demonstrated its deceitfulness. Furthermore, when sin convinces you that *you can fail to achieve* this rest and thereby lose your fellowship with God or your relationship with Him, it has demonstrated its deceitfulness.

Bottom line? When sin convinces you that this rest is an addendum to the finished work of Jesus, it has demonstrated its deceitfulness! In fact, when sin has accomplished that purpose, it has caused you to miss the rest that remains for you. Sin is indeed exceedingly deceitful when it deceives us into believing our Sabbath rest is something we must achieve to perfect the work Jesus accomplished on the cross. To say that another way, sin is exceedingly deceitful when it deceives us into believing our Sabbath rest is the fruit of our continued work rather than the fruit of His finished work!

Remember this: Jesus worked to give you rest! Whatever you do, be diligent to enter that rest; be diligent to rest in His finished work! I think the author of Hebrews states it about as clearly as it can be stated: "Therefore, let us fear lest, while a promise remains of entering His rest, any one of you should seem to have come short of it" (4:1). "Let us therefore be diligent to enter that rest, lest anyone fall through following the same example of disobedience" (4:11).

What does "following this same example of disobedience" mean? It means doing what Israel did! It is placing your trust in your ability to achieve righteousness rather than placing your trust in Jesus's ability to achieve righteousness for you. *It is viewing the Sabbath as a day you are to keep holy rather than as the person of Jesus, who is holy.* It is refusing to accept Him as your Sabbath rest. It is working to earn what He has already earned for you through His vicarious death. In a very real sense, it is placing your trust in the work that Moses started but never finished rather than placing your trust in the work Jesus both started and finished!

Sadly, the vast majority of Christians view this Sabbath rest as a day (Sunday), not the person of Jesus. For the mainline denomination (with a few exceptions), Sunday is the day this rest is to be observed. This practice comes from the Jewish interpretation of the commandment "Remember the Sabbath Day to keep it holy." If my information is correct, in an effort to interpret this commandment, the Jews developed 210 rules as to how the Sabbath Day was to be kept holy! If my memory is correct, my mother, who at the time was very legalistic in her theology, had 310 rules concerning the same matter. Playing golf on Sunday was out—period. Fishing on Sunday was out—period. Thank goodness, cutting grass on Sunday was out as well. Opening one's business on Sunday was out, with a few exceptions: restaurants, gas stations, and funeral homes. The hospital had to be closed, but it was okay for the doctor to make house calls. Of course, attending church was fine! I could go on and on, but I trust you can see the futility in this exercise of self-righteousness. No two people had the same rules, not even my own parents, and no one kept the rules they did have for any extended period of time. I guess everyone thought God grades on a curve. I can tell you this without equivocation: I was very relieved when I realized not only that Jesus is my Sabbath Rest but also that I rest in Him and in His finished work every day and all day. *Honey from the rock!*

As you remember, God did not allow Moses to lead the Israelites into the Promised Land, the land of rest, because of his own disobedience, his own lack of faith in the sufficiency of God; consequently, he could only see the land from a distance. "But the Lord said to Moses and Aaron, 'Because you have not believed Me, to treat Me as holy in the sight of the sons of Israel, therefore you shall not bring this assembly into the land which I have given them'" (Numbers 20:12). "For you shall see the land at a distance, but you shall not go there, into the land which I am giving the sons of Israel" (Deuteronomy 32:52). I see this as a mirror image of the predicament of Adam and Eve when God threw them out of the garden.

In like manner, when we place our trust in our own abilities, as did Moses when he struck the rock rather than following God's simple but clear instructions to speak to it, we, too, will see the land of rest from a distance. It will be said of us, as it was said of Israel of old—"There remains therefore a Sabbath rest for the people of God" (Hebrews 4:9).

The author of the letter to the Hebrews made this relationship between unbelief and disobedience and falling short of this rest very clear when he said this: "And to whom did He swear that they should not enter His rest, but to those who were disobedient? And so we see that they were not able to enter because of unbelief" (Hebrews 3:18–19). To be sure, those who were disobedient, those who did not believe God's provision was sufficient, failed to enter this rest because of their unbelief. Sadly, Christian believers still fail to enter this Sabbath rest because of the disobedience of unbelief. Sadly, they refuse to believe His provision is sufficient and thus continue attempting to keep Sunday holy.

You might be asking, "Why all this fuss about resting when there is so much work to be done?" The answer should be obvious, but many still see through a glass rather darkly. The truth is this: The work is finished! There is nothing left for us to do! Jesus declared it so with the words: "It is finished" (John 19:30)! The author of Hebrews stated it very clearly: "His works were finished from the foundation of the world" (Hebrews 4:3b). Again, in chapter 4, he tells us this: "For the one who has entered His rest has himself also rested from his works as God did from His" (Hebrews 4:10).

Maybe we all need to be reminded of these familiar words: "Come to Me, all who are weary and heavy-laden, and I will give you rest. Take My yoke upon you, and learn from Me, for I am gentle and humble in heart; and YOU SHALL FIND REST FOR YOUR SOULS. For My yoke is easy, and My load is light" (Matthew 11:28). Maybe this explains why the author of Hebrews was so interested in each of us entering into and remaining in our Sabbath rest.

After several readings of the aforementioned verse (Hebrews 4:10), I finally realized it tells us how to recognize those who have truly entered into God's rest; it gives us the evidence of this rest.

Look at it again: "For the one who has entered His rest has himself also rested from his works, as God did from His" (Hebrews 4:10). Some things are so obvious that we simply overlook them, and this is an excellent example. How have we missed it? Every Christian who has entered the rest that God has provided for him in Jesus *has also* rested from his works—*even as God* has rested from His works!

In other words, he is no longer attempting to do anything to add to or to take away from God's provision in Jesus. He is no longer attempting to do anything to earn what God has already provided in Jesus. To say it another way, He is simply trusting that the work Jesus finished from before the foundation of the world will be completely sufficient for his justification, sanctification, and glorification, and not only for his but also for the rest of God's elect.

Listen to John MacArthur's commentary on this subject of rest:

> The rest promised to those who believe is My rest, that is, God's rest. God's own rest from His work of creation, and the rest that He gives us in Christ are not the rest brought on by weariness or the rest of inactivity, but are the rest of finished work. His works were finished from the foundation of the world. God has finished His work. God has done it all, and for anyone who wants to enter into His finished work and to share in His rest, it available by faith. When God had finished the creation, He said (briefly paraphrasing Genesis 2), "It's done. I've made a wonderful world for man and woman. I've given them everything earthly they need, including each other, for a complete and beautiful and satisfying life. Even more importantly, they have perfect, unbroken, unmarred fellowship with Me. I can now rest; and they can rest in Me."[18]

---

[18]   Ibid., 101.

Imagine for a minute (if you can rest long enough) what it would be like to live the rest of your life resting in the glorious truth that you are in perfect and permanent relationship with God. Furthermore, imagine what it would be like never again to have to come up with some manipulation to convince God to give you another chance or that you would never again be afraid of disappointing God. Continue imagining, and imagine what it would be like to spend the remainder of your days knowing that Jesus is truly in love with *you*, regardless of your behavior. *Honey from the rock!*

Please allow me to be more specific, maybe even more personal: Can you imagine what it would be like not to feel guilty because you failed to have your quiet time, missed Sunday school and church, or did not want to attend prayer meeting? Can you imagine what it would be like not to feel guilty because you failed to witness to someone or because you were the only one who did not want to work in the soup kitchen?

Give me one more attempt: can you imagine what it would be like to live the rest of your life without feeling you are a failure because you failed to measure up to another's expectations?

If it is difficult for you to imagine any of these scenarios, in all probability it is because you do not have much confidence is Jesus's finished work. Remember this: "For the one who has entered His rest has himself rested from his works, as God did from His" (Hebrews 4:10).

I recently attended the funeral service of lady who had lived over ninety years. The minister reminded us of many of the changes that had taken place during her long life. Actually, it was quite interesting! I wonder, though, have you ever stopped to consider all the changes that have taken place since the birth of our Lord? Our forefathers would not (could not) believe the way we live today!

Can you imagine what it would be like for someone who was alive as recently as January 1, 1000, to wake up on November 1, 2000? I am not sure, but I'm willing to bet that he would spend most of the first day trying to figure out what to do with that tube of stuff that sits alongside that little brush that sits somewhere on your lavatory. What would he think when you took him to Kroger's, to a movie, or to the mall? Can you imagine what he would think when you took him to the airport in Atlanta? Can you imagine trying to get him to board one of the airplanes? I know you would blow his mind if you took him to downtown Atlanta, especially during rush hour! What would he do with a hamburger and fries!

The truth is we are mind-boggled at the changes ourselves. Things are changing so fast that we simply cannot keep up, even with computers to help us. To wake up on any given morning is to wake up to change. What was, no longer is. We have the "I can't believe it" syndrome almost every day!

My concern is this: The fast-paced lives we live simply trying to keep up with the changes that occur, not to mention all the other stressors, are stressing us to the max and even beyond the max! I am convinced stress is one of Satan's favorite tools! He uses it to cause more problems than any of us would care to know. Unfortunately, however, most people have been stressed for so long that they have come to believe stress is normal, even necessary. It is almost as if we treat it as a status symbol.

Do not be deceived! A stress-filled life is the very antithesis of the true Christian life. *Stress robs us of the rest that is ours as children of the Most High God!* It is, therefore, the enemy of physical health, the enemy of emotional health, and the enemy of spiritual health.

Are these words, *"Be still and know that I am God,"* familiar to you? Why do you think He gave us that directive? He knew from before the foundation of the world that stress would be our enemy, especially for those of us who would be alive at the beginning of the third millennium!

If you happen to be one of those who are stressed to the max, think those words over—savor them and then *do* them! *Be still* until you *know* He is God! The result will be one of the most incredible experiences you have known.

When you have been still long enough to *know* He is God, it will then become evident to you that you have been acting as if you were the slave of some other god, and it will become just as evident that you have been marching to his double-time drumbeat! My guess is that when you have been *still* long enough to *know* that He is God, you will quickly resign your membership in the *Society of the Stressed!* As a result, you will become much more like *the lilies of the field* that are marching to His drumbeat and resting in His finished work. By the way, they neither toil nor spin, yet Solomon in all of his glory was never arrayed as one of these. In other words, they live stress-free lives!

I know you know this, but allow me to remind you: In all of these years and in all of this change, Jesus has remained the same. He is the same yesterday, today, and forever! Even when our children's, children's children are walking around on this earth (should He tarry that long), He will be the same. Talk about stress free! He has no reason to be stressed; after all, He is not trying to measure up to someone's unrealistic expectations or to climb some corporate ladder. He is not trying to become a zillionaire or trying to figure out how to pay His debts (He doesn't have any). He is not trying to live from paycheck to paycheck or work for some employer who is more interested in the bottom line than the people who work for him. He is not even trying to figure out how to live forever. The truth is He is not trying—period! He simply is—period! I guess one could say He neither toils nor spins. He simply rests and rests and rests. Maybe this is why we are called human *be*ings.

I said all of that so I could say this: His life is the true Christian life, and His lifestyle is the only lifestyle worth living—period! If you are tired of striving, I suggest that you heed the call of His life and of His lifestyle. "Come to Me, all who are weary and heavy-laden, and I will give you rest" (Mathew 11:28). That is correct—*rest*! To repeat some of the words of the author of Hebrews: "There remains, therefore, a Sabbath rest for the people of God" (Hebrews 4:9). I think one could say it this way: there remains, therefore, a stress-free life (neither toiling nor spinning) for the people of God.

Would you like to receive this incredible gift of rest that God has for provided for you in Jesus and begin resting in His life and in His lifestyle—*stress free*? It really is the Christian way of life! It is what He had in mind for you from the beginning.

Remember, Solomon in all of his glory never even came close to knowing the lifestyle of those who have learned to rest in His finished work, who refuse to get caught up in all the *toiling* and *spinning* of life! If my memory serves me correctly, Jesus compared these to the lilies of the field. "Observe how the lilies of the field grow; they do not toil nor do they spin, yet I say to you that even Solomon in all his glory did not clothe himself like one of these" (Matthew 6:28b–29).

Before I leave this section, I want to say something about the modern-day concept of evangelism. I would like to think that every Christian believes God has long since rested from His *finished* work concerning evangelism. Unfortunately, however, most live as if they believe He is still busy trying to figure out how to gather all the lost into His family; consequently, most have this compelling urge to help Him finish this tremendous task. It is obvious that many sincerely believe God needs them to help Him reach the lost. Some are so convinced of this that they find themselves on foreign mission fields or in the pastorate, devoting entire lifetimes to that relentless pursuit.

I will never forget an e-mail I received, early one Sunday morning from a missionary in Africa. His e-mail had this urgent message: "Please pray for 'John,' as he is deathly sick; thousands of Africans will die and go to hell if he dies." I thought to myself, *Gosh, I am so thankful that burden in not on my shoulders!*

Yes, I believe every sincere believer has a keen interest in seeing the lost come to know Jesus. To be sure, the apostle Paul did! These are his words:

> I am telling the truth in Christ, I am not lying, my
> conscience bearing me witness in the Holy Spirit, that
> I have great sorrow and unceasing grief in my heart.
> For I could wish that I myself were accursed, separated

from Christ for the sake of my brethren, my kinsmen
according to the flesh. (Romans 9:1–3)

To say you love Jesus but do not have a strong interest in seeing
others come to know Him is an oxymoron. However, I am afraid we
have failed to realize that the burden of evangelism is on the Holy
Spirit, not on us. Truthfully, evangelism has long since become a
thing of great pride rather than a thing of humility.

If you were to take a look at Jesus's style of evangelism, you
would quickly realize He would never pass Evangelism 101 in today's
seminaries. He was under no stress whatsoever to reach the lost;
instead, He was confident He would not lose even one of those the
Father gave to Him. I will remind you that He never mentioned
anything about a sinner's prayer or an altar call or a Tuesday-evening
visitation program. He simply went about loving His Father and
loving people. His *method* worked while He rested in His Father's
predetermined plan! Listen to what He said: "Of those whom Thou
hast given Me I lost not one" (John 18:9b). *Honey from the rock!*

Listen, my dear friend, somewhere, long before the world ever
was, God finished the work that was necessary for the redemption
of His elect. These words of Jesus as He hung on the cross say that
as clearly as anyone could say it; after all, He is the Savior/Redeemer:
"It is finished" (John 19:30)! The Savior has finished His work, and
because He is God, He finished His work *before* the foundation
of the world! The work is truly finished, and the party has begun!
Honey from the rock!

Does this mean we do nothing? Absolutely not! It does mean,
however, that our motivation for doing what we do needs to change
from self-righteous works to the works that He prepared beforehand
that we might walk in them. "For we are His workmanship, created
in Christ Jesus for good works, which God prepared beforehand,
that we should walk in them" (Ephesians 2:10).

As you read these quotes from Robert Capon, listen carefully to
the words, as I think they speak very clearly:

Jesus cares only about whether people are someplace where trust alone can get them, not about whether they can claim to have worked their way there by noble efforts ... the Gospel is not some self-improvement scheme devised by a God who holds back on us till He sees the improvements. Above all, Jesus wants to make sure we understand He doesn't care a fig about our precious results. It doesn't even make a difference to Him if we're solid brass bastards, because "while we were still sinners, Christ died for the ungodly" ... God isn't fair: if He were, we'd all be in the soup. God is good: crazy, stark-staring-bonkers good.[19]

Questions for Study

1. When Jesus finished His work, He sat down. Why?

2. Define "Sabbath rest."

3. Is this rest an essential ingredient in or an addendum to our justification?

4. Is there something we must do to finish Jesus's work?

---

[19] Robert Farrar Capon, *The Mystery of Christ: and Why We Don't Get It* (Grand Rapids, MI: William B. Eerdmans Publishing Company, 1993), 90-91.

5. Why do so many Christians fall short of entering into this Sabbath rest?

6. What is the result of believers falling short of this Sabbath rest?

7. What is the warning the author gives to his readers concerning this Sabbath rest?

8. Every Christian actually lives every moment of every day in the Sabbath rest. True or false?

9. Describe what the scriptures mean by the "deceitfulness of sin."

10. What does "following this same example of disobedience" mean?

11. How can we recognize one who has truly entered into the Sabbath rest?

12. Is God in some kind of time crunch regarding evangelism and therefore needs our help to gather His family together?

13. What is the antithesis of rest?

11

—❦—

FAITH WITHOUT WORKS

Having said quite a bit about resting, I do want to make some comments about working. I do so because I am aware that most of you are already stressing over James's comment about faith and works. "Just as the body without the spirit is dead, so also faith without works is dead" (James 2:26). Some of you are probably thinking I am implying those who embrace this teaching regarding resting are free to do nothing but sit in their rockers and drink mint juleps. The fact is that is true. You really are free to sit in your rocker and drink mint juleps, if you so choose. However, those who truly embrace the gospel never, ever take that position.

Those who embrace the true gospel are finally free from the tyranny of the law and are, therefore, actually able to do the *good* works that God prepared beforehand for them. "For we are His workmanship, created in Christ Jesus for good works, which God prepared beforehand, that we should walk in them" (Ephesians 2:1). Just for the record: it is impossible for anyone to do any of these good works until he is free from the tyranny of the law, as that tyrannical authority poisons his motivation. Consequently, the best of his efforts are only works of the flesh, which can never please God.

The question now, I suppose, is this: Is it possible to have genuine faith—the faith that is a gift from God, the faith that causes us to believe the one, true gospel—without it being accompanied by good works? The answer is a resounding no. The fact is the only people who do good works, the works God prepared beforehand for us to walk in, are those who have embraced the one, true gospel and are thereby freed from the tyranny of the law.

A Personal Story

I have been working since I was about fourteen years old. For some reason, my father believed work was a noble thing. He worked, and he saw to it that I worked. Believe it or not, some of it was hard work, as in very hard work. He thought nothing of working from the rising of the sun to the setting of the same, and all through the following night, if necessary. It was often necessary, as he owned a funeral home in addition to a general mercantile store.

His motivation was very clear: he worked to provide for his family. He never complained about it, not once to my knowledge. No work was beneath his dignity. Some might have called him a workaholic, but I beg to differ. Workaholics have a different motivation than my father's. Their motivation is insecurity; his was love.

I carefully watched him without even knowing that I was. In many ways, I became what I saw. I, too, believe work is a noble thing. Laziness has never appealed to me, and neither have lazy people. Some of those who knew me in my younger years might have called me a workaholic, and to be honest, they would have been correct, at least to some degree. I say that because I know a significant part of my motivation was my desire to please my father.

Interestingly, apart from two specific exceptions, he never indicated he was not pleased with me. No one has ever complimented me as much as he did. He told me he was proud of me countless times, far too many for me to remember. Ironically, even though I never doubted his love for me, I pressed on to please him.

Apart from the two aforementioned exceptions, I never did anything that I thought would disappoint him. Pleasing him was the driving motivation of my life. That motivation, however, changed dramatically when I realized he loved me because I was his son, not because I tried so hard to please him. Thankfully that was long before he died on January 9, 1994.

When my motivation changed, I didn't stop working and sit in my rocker drinking mint juleps. I continued to work, but my reason for working changed. This was when our business relationship ended and I entered the ministry. I was finally free to do the work God prepared beforehand for me to walk in and in so doing, to honor not only my earthly father but also my heavenly Father.

Interestingly, I had to become a father before I could understand what I had theretofore misunderstood. Love carries no conditions; true love is one-way love. When I became a father, I got a glimpse of what that really means. You see, I wanted to please my father because I wanted his love. The fact is I already had his love, and it came without any conditions. It was not in any way dependent upon my responses or my actions.

I tell you that story because it reminds me of the story of so many of today's Christians. They work, but the works they do are nothing more than works of the flesh because their motivation is fear, not faith—a self-centered pursuit, indeed.

Robert Farrar Capon said it this way:

> Jesus didn't say He came to judge sinners, or even to turn them into non-sinners; He makes it quite clear that His salvation works by grace through faith, not by frightening people into getting their act together. [20]

---

[20] Ibid., 18.

Questions for Study

1. Is it possible for one to have genuine faith in Jesus and in His finished work without doing the good works God prepared beforehand for us?

2. How can we know the works we do are actually good works?

3. Do our works, whether they are works of the flesh or good works, do anything to earn right standing with God?

4. Do works, whether they are works of the flesh or good works, impress God at all?

5. What must happen before anyone can do the good works God prepared for us?

6. What is a workaholic?

7. If fear is motivating us, what kind of works will we inevitably do?

12

THE ALTAR CALL

Back in my early days as a Christian, the invitation or altar call was a vital part of the preaching of the gospel; in fact, for one to preach a sermon without giving an invitation was equal to being a heretic. The purpose of the invitation was to urge sinners to come to the mourner's bench and be saved or to come and be sanctified, usually some of both. Oftentimes, because of their importance, the preachers would extend these altar calls for quite a while. Most of them had their favorite hymns of invitation, such as "Just As I Am," "Softly and Tenderly," "The Savior is Waiting," "Don't Go Away without Jesus," and of course, "I Surrender All."

I can remember the waiting as these preachers would extend these invitations through all the verses of several songs, and I can remember the mourners walking forward "to surrender all," or "not to keep the Savior waiting." To be honest, I became one of these preachers, and to this day, I deeply regret it. Thankfully, the Holy Spirit changed my mind-set before I did too much damage, although any damage is too much.

Yes, I do know God used some of these invitations to draw some of His elect unto Himself; however, His drawing probably had more to do with the "foolishness of the message preached" than it had to do with the invitation. "Since in the wisdom of God the world through its wisdom did not come to know God, God was well-pleased through the foolishness of the message preached to save those who believe" (1 Corinthians 1:21).

You see, the church as I knew it was poised to reach the masses for Jesus, and it had a keen sense of urgency about doing it. Well, some of them were. It was apparent God was having a difficult time gathering His family, so He came begging for our help. What I did not know was this: God intended the gospel for His elect, not for the masses, and He was certainly in no dilemma regarding the gathering of His elect family. Now that I think about it, none of the other preachers knew it either, or if they did, they kept it hidden quite well.

Anyway, as God continued to reveal Himself to me, as I continued to think for myself, I realized God really did not need me, or anyone else for that matter, to help Him gather His elect family, and He was not in some kind of time crunch about getting it done. The message to me was clear—very clear: You are to preach the gospel—period. I will cause the Holy Spirit to draw My elect to Me, through the *foolishness* of the message you preach. Well, that was humbling! "I am not ashamed of the gospel, for it is the power of God for salvation for everyone who believer" (Romans 1:16). *Honey from the rock!*

At any rate, that ended my days of giving invitations and altar calls. I must admit, however, that on those rare occasions when He has told me to give an invitation, I did just that; however, it did not take sixteen verses of "Just As I Am" to get the job done—not even five.

In my mind, inviting folks to come to Jesus is a very good thing to do. How could anyone who has been born of the Spirit of God do otherwise? It took me a few years, however, to see the one, true invitation, and it is this: the holy Eucharist.

Yes, I know you are probably thinking the holy Eucharist cannot be an invitation for sinners to come to Jesus because the table is not for them. You are probably even thinking that it is *only* for those who have somehow managed to get things right with God. Well, the table is for believers only; however, I want to encourage you to continue reading, as you might just hear a fresh truth.

The following is the information I convey to every person who enters the doors of the church I presently pastor—Grace Christian Fellowship:

> As we welcome you to Grace Christian Fellowship, we want to call your attention to the fact that the table is prepared for the celebration of the holy Eucharist— the Lord's Supper. Because we believe the eating of the bread and the drinking of the wine, when preceded by the proclamation of the Word of God, provides spiritual nourishment for our thirsty and hungry souls, we celebrate this supper frequently—every time the gospel is proclaimed.
>
> Jesus was unmistakably clear in identifying the unleavened bread with His body—"Take eat; this is My body" (Matthew 26:26). He was just as clear in identifying the wine with His blood: "Drink from it all of you; for this is My blood of the covenant, which is poured out for many for forgiveness of sins" (Matthew 26:27–28). In light of this, we believe that when a believer eats the bread and drinks the wine within the setting of the proclaimed Word of God, the Holy Spirit miraculously causes the bread and wine (the signs) to actually become what they signify—the body and blood of Christ—and thereby, the signs become genuine spiritual nourishment for the believer.
>
> Obviously, we view the signs as being much more than mere symbols; however, we do not go to the other

extreme and view them as being, in and of themselves, the body and blood of Jesus—transubstantiation.

Our position is this: The signs (bread and wine) become what they signify (the body and blood of Jesus) when and only when the believer receives them—that is, when the believer actually eats the bread and drinks the wine. It must, however, be noted that this miracle is accomplished by the work of the Holy Spirit and only by His work. In fact, apart from the Word of God and the work of the Holy Spirit, the bread and wine are just that—bread and wine; however, when a believer receives the bread and wine, joined with the Word and the Holy Spirit, a miracle happens. At that moment, the bread and wine become within the life of the believer what they signify: the body and blood of Jesus—true food and true drink (genuine spiritual nourishment).

When Jesus inaugurated this supper, He used unleavened bread (not saltine crackers or loaf bread), and He used wine (not grape juice). Since it is our purpose to be faithful to His example, we want you to be aware that the bread is unleavened bread and the wine is wine—fermented juice of grapes.

We encourage you as a believer to partake of the signs, and we also encourage you to trust that when you do, the Holy Spirit will cause the signs to actually become what they signify—the body and blood of Jesus; Christ in you—true drink and true food.

Yes, I realize that does not sound like an invitation to sinners; however, when one of God's elect, one who has not yet been made aware that he is one of God's elect, is sitting in the congregation being drawn to Jesus through the foolishness of the message preached, it becomes quite an attraction! "For as often as you eat this bread and drink the cup, you proclaim the Lord's death until He comes" (1 Corinthians 11:26).

It would be improper for me to conclude this section without giving you John Calvin's comments regarding this supper:

> It seems to me that a simple and proper definition would be to say that it is an outward sign by which the Lord seals on our consciences the promises of His good will toward us in order to sustain the weakness of our faith; and we in turn attest our piety toward Him in the presence of the Lord and of His angels and before men. Here is another briefer definition: one may call it a testimony of divine grace toward us, confirmed by an outward sign, with mutual attestation of our piety toward Him. Whichever of these definitions you may choose, it does not differ in meaning from that of Augustine, who teaches that a sacrament is "a visible sign of a sacred thing," or "a visible form of an invisible grace," but it better and more clearly explains the thing itself.[21]

---

[21] John Calvin, *Institutes of the Christian Religion,* ed. John T. McNeill, trans. Ford Lewis Battles, Library of Christian Classics (Philadelphia: Westminster, 1960), 4.14.1.

Questions for Study

1. In the minds of some, the invitation is all-important. Why?

2. What does God use to attract sinners other than the obvious—the Holy Spirit?

3. Why is it a good thing to invite folk to Jesus?

4. What is the most effective invitation? Explain.

13

CONCERNING GOD'S ELECT

Because I am keenly aware of the stigma many have placed upon such terms as *choice, election, foreknowledge*, and *predestination*, I am compelled to at the very least offer some passages from the scriptures where these terms are used. Hopefully you will carefully read them with the purpose of knowing truth.

However, before I offer the passages, I want to allow you the opportunity to read what Loraine Boettner had to say about predestination:

> In the minds of most people the doctrine of Predestination and Calvinism are practically synonymous terms. This, however, should not be the case, and the too close identification of the two has doubtless done much to prejudice many people against the Calvinistic system ... The doctrine of Predestination has been made the subject of almost endless discussion, much of which, it must be admitted, was for the purpose of softening its outlines or of explaining it away ... There is probably no subject that has occupied more of the attention of intelligent men in every age. It has been most fully discussed in all of its bearings, philosophical, theological, and

practical; and if there be any subject of speculation with respect to which we are warranted in saying that it has been exhausted, it is this.[22]

> For you are a holy people to the Lord your God; the Lord your God has chosen you to be a people for His own possession out of all the peoples who are on the face of the earth. The Lord did not set His love on you nor choose you because you were more in number than any of the peoples, for you were the fewest of all peoples, but because the Lord loved you and kept the oath which He swore to your forefathers, the Lord brought you out by a mighty hand, and redeemed you from the house of slavery, from the hand of Pharaoh king of Egypt. (Deuteronomy 7:6–8)

Yes, this is specifically concerning Israel; however, even a casual look at Romans 11 will tell you that we have been grafted into the True Vine—true Jews indeed. "And when the Gentiles heard this, they began rejoicing and glorifying the word of the Lord; and *as many as had been appointed to eternal life believed*" (Acts 13:48, emphasis mine). In my humble opinion, this is irrefutable evidence that God has called and appointed a group of people to believe the unbelievable gospel and as a result, become His elect people.

> For whom He foreknew; He also predestined to become conformed to the image of His Son, that He might be the first-born among many brethren; and whom He predestined, these He also called; and whom He called, these He also justified; and whom He justified, these He also glorified. (Romans 8:29–30)

---

[22] Loraine Boettner, *The Reformed Doctrine of Predestination* (Presbyterian and Reformed Publishing Company: Phillipsburg, NJ, 1932), 7.

Unless you are a universalist and believe that everyone will be justified and glorified, you must take the position that God foreknew, predestined, called, justified, and glorified an elect group of people to be His children. Notice that those He called, He also justified. Did He call everyone and thus justify and glorify everyone, or did He call a group to whom He chose to show mercy and justify and glorify them? If you believe in both heaven and hell, then the answer is the latter, not the former. By the way, notice the tense of the verbs.

> Blessed be the God and Father of our Lord Jesus Christ, who has blessed us with every spiritual blessing in the heavenly places in Christ, *just as He chose us in Him before the foundation of the world,* that we should be holy and blameless before Him. (Ephesians 1:3–4, emphasis mine).

Can it be any clearer? God chose us before the foundation of the world! How cool is that? Notice that He didn't simply choose us, but He chose us to be holy and blameless before Him! *Honey from the rock, indeed!*

> Blessed be the God and Father of our Lord Jesus Christ, who according to His great *mercy has caused us to be born again* to a living hope through the resurrection of Jesus Christ from the dead, to obtain an inheritance which is imperishable and undefiled and will not fade away, reserved in heaven for you, who are protected by the power of God through faith for a salvation ready to be revealed in the last time. (1 Peter 1:3–5, emphasis mine)

Obviously, if God actually caused some to be born again, well, surely that is a no-brainer. *"As those who have been chosen of God, holy and beloved*, put on a heart of compassion, kindness, humility, gentleness and patience" (Colossians 3:12, emphasis mine). Again, can it be any clearer? I do not think so.

> What then? That which Israel is seeking for, it has not obtained, *but those who were chosen obtained it*, and the rest were hardened; just as it is written, "God gave them a spirit of stupor, eyes to see not and ears to hear not, down to this very day." (Romans 11:7–9)

Surely that is enough evidence to convince you that God really is sovereign over all, even over justification and glorification. If you think not, please reread the passages with an open mind and listen to what the Sprit says. It really is okay for God to be sovereign over all. I wouldn't want it any other way.

This does lead me to say something about prayer. Over the years, I have noticed that most of us (probably all of us!) spend most of our prayer time asking God for something we fear He is going to withhold from us. To say that another way, we spend most of our prayer time attempting to talk God into changing His mind to accommodate our desires. Even Jesus did this for a brief period in the garden of Gethsemane—the place of crushing—when He was sweating drops of blood and saying, "If if is possible, let this cup pass from Me; nevertheless, not My will but Yours be done." I can assure you that He came to that "nevertheless" place much more quickly than any of us would have.

You see, when you truly believe God is love, all-powerful, and sovereign over all, you no longer feel the need to talk Him into changing His mind about anything. Maybe prayer has more to do His bringing us to our own nevertheless place than it has to do with our getting something from Him—something that we think we cannot live without, not for long anyway.

Questions for Study

1. Why do you think so many people struggle with the terms *choice, election, foreknowledge,* and *predestination*?

2. Did God call everyone and then leave the choice to respond positively up to them, or did God only call a particular group of people and guarantee their justification?

3. Did God's prescience determine His choice in election?

4. Paul tells us in Romans 9 that God shows mercy to whom He chooses to show mercy, and He hardens whom He chooses to harden. Is that fair?

5. Do you really want God to be fair?

6. What about your prayer life?

14

CONCERNING OUR
SPIRITUAL INHERITANCE

He made known to us the mystery of His will, according to His kind intention which He purposed in Him with a view to an administration suitable to the fullness of the times, that is, the summing up of all things in Christ, things in the heavens and things upon the earth. In Him also *we have received an inheritance*, having been predestined according to His purpose who works all things after the counsel of His will, to the end that we who were the first to hope in Christ should be to the praise of His glory. (Ephesians 1:9–12, emphasis mine)

Blessed be the God and Father of our Lord Jesus Christ, who according to His great mercy has caused us to be born again to a living hope through the resurrection of Jesus Christ from the dead, *to obtain an inheritance* which is imperishable and undefiled and will not fade away, reserved in Heaven for you who are protected by the power of God through faith for a salvation ready to be revealed in the last time. (1 Peter 1:3–5, emphasis mine)

Very specifically, what is this inheritance? It is the life of Jesus! Just to set the record straight: God, from the foundation of the world, made you an heir of His estate, a joint-heir with Jesus. Listen to these words of Paul:

> He made known to us the mystery of His will, according to His kind intention which He purposed in Him with a view to an administration suitable to the fullness of the times, that is, the summing up of all things in Christ, things in the heavens and things upon the earth. *In Him also we have obtained an inheritance,* having been predestined according to His purpose who works all things after the counsel of His will, to the end that we who were the first to hope in Christ should be to the praise of His glory. (Ephesians 1:9–12, emphasis mine) (See also Colossians 1:12 and 1 Peter 1:3–5.)

As you know, before *anyone* could receive this inheritance, God had to die, and He did in the person of His only begotten Son, Jesus. Because God exists in three persons—Father, Son, and Holy Spirit—He could do this and yet live! Furthermore, because Jesus rose from the dead, He became an heir to this inheritance; we, then, are joint-heirs with Jesus to God's estate! We have indeed received an inheritance—an incredible inheritance! Take a minute and think about that, as it is quite overwhelming.

Whatever else might be ours, nothing can compare to the fact that, *above everything else, it is the life of Jesus that we have received.* We must never lose sight of that single truth because in it we find many benefits, benefits that will forever change our lives *if* we *receive* them. To use the words of Martyn Lloyd-Jones:

> In Christ Jew and Gentile are not only fellow-heirs together; still more wonderful, they are joint-heirs with Christ. That is the statement of the Apostle in

his Epistle to the Romans in chapter 8, verse 17—"If Children, then heirs; heirs of God, and (therefore) joint-heirs with Christ." We are "in Him," we belong to Him, and therefore we are joint-heirs with Him— joint-heirs with one another and joint-heirs with Him. Everything is in Christ. Were we to grasp this as we should we would not only be the happiest people on the face of the earth, we would also "rejoice with joy unspeakable, and full of glory." We would do so because with Paul we would realize that we have an interest in all this, we have a stake in it; we belong to the people who are going to share it.[23]

Before I move on with the specifics of the benefits of our inheritance, there are several things I want to emphasize:

(1) If you want to benefit from this inheritance while you are walking around on this earth, *you must receive it.* If you allow the error you have been taught to keep you from receiving this inheritance, it will not be of much benefit to you. If you allow what you are able to reason as truth to prevent you from receiving this inheritance, it will not be of much benefit to you. If you allow your mother's or father's rejection of you to prevent you from receiving this inheritance, it will not be of much benefit to you. To be sure, one of the significant blessings of this inheritance is life after death; however, there are many benefits for us while we sojourn here, *if we receive them.*

(2) This inheritance guarantees your eternal, dues-paid-in-full membership in the new covenant. As the result of God's irresistible invitation, you are a bona fide member of the

---

23 D. Martyn Lloyd-Jones, *God's Ultimate Purpose: An Exposition of Ephesians 1* (Grand Rapids, MI: Baker Book House: 1978), 218.

new covenant; old things have indeed passed away, and new things have come!

Whatever one might say about the importance of the old covenant, this is what the scriptures have to say: "When He said, 'A new covenant,' He has made the first obsolete. But whatever is becoming obsolete and growing old is ready to disappear" (Hebrews 8:13). "Then He said, 'Behold, I have come to do Thy will.' He takes away the first in order to establish the second" (Hebrews 10:9).

Suggestion: Read Hebrews 9 for more information.

(3) One of the evidences that you have truly received this inheritance is the fact that you never attempt to abuse it or misuse it. As you know, many people who receive a physical inheritance (i.e., money, land, houses, etc.) abuse and/or misuse it. After six months or a year, many don't have any of it left. In other words, it never really had any significant value to them, so they squandered it.

There are others, however, who purpose to hoard it; consequently, it never benefits them. Its value somehow becomes too valuable.

Every believer is a joint-heir with Jesus to this incredible spiritual inheritance, but sadly many abuse it and misuse it, and they do so because they have never really received it. The fact is these people attempt to have it both ways: to keep one foot in the old covenant and the other in the new covenant; to eat from both trees.

With all of that said, allow me to share with you some truths that will assist you in receiving your inheritance:

(1) You no longer bear the burden of your sins, as Jesus bore your sins in His body on the cross (i.e., you are free from sin—its power, its guilt, its penalty, and its condemnation!). "And *He Himself bore our sins in His body on the cross,* that we might die to sin and live to righteousness, for by His wounds you were healed" (1 Peter 2:24, emphasis mine). "For if we have become united with Him in the likeness of His death, certainly we shall be also in the likeness of His resurrection, knowing this, *that our old self was crucified with Him, that our body of sin might be done away with, that we should no longer be slaves to sin, for he who has died is freed from sin"* (Romans 6:5–7, emphasis mine).

(2) Your sin debt—past, present, and future—has been paid in full. "And when you were dead in your transgressions and the uncircumcision of your flesh, He made you alive together with Him, *having forgiven us all our transgressions, having canceled out the certificate of debt* consisting of decrees against us and which was hostile to us, and *He has taken it out of the way, having nailed it to the cross"* (Colossians 2:13–14, emphasis mine).

My dear friend, as far as God is concerned, you are forever debt free, and you are because Jesus paid your debt for you—a debt you could have never paid. He paid it all! You contributed absolutely nothing, and for good reason—you had nothing to contribute!

(3) You are forgiven—forever forgiven! Period! Never again do you have to beg God to forgive you, as He has already done so—permanently.

(4) Your body of flesh has been removed as the result of the circumcision of Christ. "And in Him you were also circumcised with a circumcision made without hands, *in the*

removal of the body of the flesh by the circumcision of Christ" (Colossians 2:1, emphasis mine).

The Jewish teachers insisted on the necessity of the literal circumcision to be a true Jew, and hence, this subject is so often introduced into the writings of Paul. He went to great pains to show that, by believing in Christ, all was obtained that was required for salvation.

Circumcision was an ordinance that indicated that all sin was to be cut off or renounced, and he who was circumcised was to be devoted to God and to a holy life. All this, the apostle says, was obtained by the gospel, and consequently, those who believe have all that was denoted by the ancient rite of circumcision, even more—much more. What Christians obtain, moreover, relates to the heart; it was not a mere ordinance pertaining to the flesh. By the circumcision of Christ, not by the fact that Christ was circumcised, our body of flesh *has been* removed.

Why is this important? It is because otherwise you would find yourself in the same position as the religious—trying to wage war against that which has been removed and discarded, namely the flesh.

(5) You are the righteousness of God in Christ, irrespective of your behavior. "He made Him who knew no sin *to be sin on our behalf, that we might become the righteousness of God in Him*" (2 Corinthians 5:21, emphasis mine).

Because He became sin on our behalf: (1) we are as righteous as He is righteous and (2) that is without respect to our behavior—past, present, or future.

15

THE BENEFITS AND BLESSINGS
OF YOUR INHERITANCE

For many years, I was involved in funeral service. During that time, I had the opportunity to observe how people respond to the possibility of receiving an inheritance, not to mention those who knew they were about to receive one. To be sure, with few exceptions, the reading of the last will and testament was of utmost importance. There was never any problem getting the heirs to assemble for that reading—never. Without exception, the heirs wanted to know what was left to them, and once they knew, they wanted to benefit from it immediately.

As strange as it might seem, most Christians have no idea they are heirs of God's estate, even joint-heirs with Jesus, and the few who do know seem to have very little interest in knowing about their inheritance. It seems they are too busy trying to earn what God has bestowed upon them as a gift to recognize that He has already gifted them with everything they need for life and for godliness. "Grace and peace be multiplied to you in the knowledge of God and of Jesus our Lord; seeing that His divine power has granted to us everything pertaining to life and godliness; through the true knowledge of Him who called us by His own glory and excellence" (2 Peter 1:2–3). *Honey from the rock!*

Sadly, of those who are aware they are joint-heirs with Jesus, most have no idea of its significance and value, and they have been taught to believe benefitting from it requires that they earn the privilege. Thankfully, it has a value that is beyond description, and it is a gift of grace (i.e., it is not for sale).

Below I am giving you several of the benefits and blessings that are yours as a bona fide member of the new covenant—the covenant of lavish grace (a.k.a., one-way love). As you read over them, purpose in your heart to receive them, even though they will probably seem too good to be true. To be sure, He became poor that we might become rich! *Honey from the rock, and then some!*

1. *Meeting the requirements of the Ten Commandments need no longer be a stressor for you* because God did for you what the law could not do for you, as is evidenced by this: "For what the Law could not do, weak as it was through the flesh, God did: sending His own Son in the likeness of sinful flesh and as an offering for sin, *He condemned sin in the flesh, in order that the requirement of the Law might be fulfilled in us,* who do not walk according to the flesh, but according to the Spirit" (Romans 8:3–4, emphasis mine).

   In other words, as a bona fide member of the new covenant, you can cease striving to meet the requirements of the Ten Commandments because Jesus satisfied the law's requirement for you, namely that sin be punished by death.

2. *Living in a continued state of forgiveness need no longer be a stressor for you* because God has chosen to make you perfect—forever perfect, as is evidenced by this: "By this will *we have been sanctified* through the offering of the body of Jesus Christ once for all. And every Priest stands daily ministering and offering time after time the same sacrifices, which can never take away sins; but He, having offered one

sacrifice for sins for all time, sat down at the right hand of God, waiting from that time onward until His enemies be made a footstool for His feet. *For by one offering He has perfected for all time those who are sanctified"* (Hebrews 10:10–14, emphasis mine).

In other words, because of the offering of the body of Jesus as the sacrifice for sin—His once-for-all-time death—the penalty for every sin you will commit during your entire lifetime has been paid in full. As a result, you are holy and perfect and consequently forever forgiven.

This is what Paul had to say: "And when you were dead in your transgressions and the uncircumcision of your flesh, He made you alive together with Him having forgiven us all our transgressions, having canceled out the certificate of debt, consisting of decrees against us and which was hostile to us; and He has taken it out of the way, having nailed it to the cross" (Colossians 2:13–14).

3. *Striving to get to heaven need no longer be a stressor for you* because God has chosen to give you a seat on the same return flight Jesus took when He ascended back to heaven, as is evidenced by this: "But God being rich in mercy, because of his great love with which He loved us, even when we were dead in our transgressions, made us alive together with Christ (by grace you have been saved), and raised us up with Him, and seated us with Him in the heavenly places, in Christ Jesus" (Ephesians 2:4–6).

In other words, you are already in heaven and comfortably seated at God's right hand in Jesus, even better than a front-row seat!

4. *Facing God at the great white throne judgment and having Him reveal to everyone the secrets of your life need no longer be a stressor for you* because He has chosen not to give you what you deserve but to set you free from all judgment and condemnation, as is evidenced by this: "There is therefore now no *condemnation for those who are in Christ Jesus*. For the law of the Spirit of life in Christ Jesus has set us free from the law of sin and death" (Romans 8:1–2, emphasis mine). Not to mention that He chose never to remember your sins again, as is evidenced by this: "And their sins and their lawless deeds I will remember no more" (Hebrews 10:17).

   In other words, God chose to provide a scapegoat for you and for your sins in the Person of Jesus. Amazingly, Jesus took your record, your certificate of debt, upon Himself, and even more amazingly, He gave you His record, His spotless, blemish-free, perfect record. Consequently, God has already judged Jesus guilty of your sins, and as a result, He has judged you righteous—as righteous as Jesus is righteous! At the great white throne judgment, God will reveal only Jesus's record!

5. *Striving to maintain your relationship with God so He will not distance Himself from you by breaking fellowship with you or by severing you from Himself altogether need no longer be a stressor for you.* Why? He chose for the success of the new covenant, unlike the success of the old covenant, to be dependent upon Jesus, as is evidenced by these passages: (1) "In Him, you also, after listening to the message of truth, the gospel of your salvation—having also believed, you were sealed in Him with the Holy Spirit of promise, who is given as a pledge of our inheritance, with a view to the redemption of God's own possession, to the praise of His glory" (Ephesians 1:13–14). (2) "And for this reason He is the mediator of a

new covenant, in order that since a death has taken place for the redemption of the transgressions that were committed under the first covenant, those who have been called may receive the promise of the eternal inheritance. For where a covenant is, there must of necessity be the death of the one who made it" (Hebrews 9:15–16).

In other words, the success of the new covenant depends upon Jesus, not you. Devotions, solitude, prayer, repentance, confession, etc., can be very beneficial, provided that you do not practice them in an effort to keep your end of the covenant and thereby to help to maintain the relationship. Jesus is your guarantee that this marriage will last eternally! Cease striving and rest in Him.

6. *Striving to stop sinning, to overcome the power of sin in your life need no longer be a stressor for you* because God chose to break the power sin had over you by releasing you from the law—the law of Moses, the Ten Commandments, the law of sin and death, the ministry of death, the ministry of condemnation—as is evidenced by these passages: (1) "For sin shall not be master over you, for you are not under law, but under grace" (Romans 6:14). (2) "Christ redeemed us from the curse of the Law, having become a curse for us—for it is written, 'Cursed is everyone who hangs on a tree'"(Galatians 3:13).

In other words, through Jesus's death, God severed you from the very thing that gave sin its power, namely the law. "While we were in the flesh, the sinful passions, which were aroused by the Law, were at work in the members of our body to bear fruit for death. But now we have been released from the Law, having died to that by which we were bound, so that we serve in newness of the Spirit and not in oldness of the letter" (Romans 7:5–6). "The sting of death is sin, and the power of sin is the law; but thanks be to God, who gives us the victory through our Lord Jesus Christ" (1 Corinthians 15:56). Consequently, sin has no power over your life, unless, of course, you decide to give it power by placing yourself under the law.

7. *Hiding from God's presence need no longer be a stressor for you,* even when your behavior is most despicable, because God chose to give to you unconditional access into His presence, as is evidenced by this: "Since therefore, brethren, we have confidence to enter the holy place by the blood of Jesus, by a new and living way which He inaugurated for us through the veil, that is, His flesh, and since we have a great high priest over the house of God, *let us draw near* with a sincere heart in full assurance of faith, having our hearts sprinkled clean from an evil conscience and our bodies washed with pure water" (Hebrews 10:19–22, emphasis mine).

In other words, you can now feel comfortable in God's presence, even when you are doing the most despicable sin you can imagine. Never again do you have to hide from Him! As you remember, Adam and Eve had reason to hide because they owned their own sin. You, however, have no reason to hide because Jesus has already taken ownership of your sin (1 Peter 2:24), and God punished Him to the full extent of the law's requirement—death. Boldly, confidently, and unashamedly, run to Him! His arms are open wide to receive you!

8. *Striving to live by a list of religious rules need no longer be a stressor for you* because Jesus sent the Holy Spirit to live in you as your guide and teacher, as is evidenced by this: "And I will ask the Father, and He will give you another Helper,

that He may be with you forever; that is the Spirit of Truth, whom the world cannot receive, because it does not behold Him or know Him, but you know Him because He abides with you, and will be in you. But the Helper, the Holy Spirit, whom the Father will send in My name, He will teach you all things, and bring to your remembrance all that I said to you" (John 14:16–17; 26).

In other words, you can now wake up each morning thoroughly convinced that the Holy Spirit will be your guide and teacher as you journey through your day. *Caution:* Even though in your mind you have the correct list of dos and don'ts, please do not think that you need to keep it for future reference; instead, get rid of it. Do not merely throw it away; burn it, for fear that someone else might find it and attempt to use it.

9. *Striving to maintain control of your life as well as the lives of others need no longer be a stressor for you* because God is in control of everyone and everything, as is evidenced by this: "And we know that *God causes all things to work together for good* to those who love God, to those who are the called according to His purpose" (Romans 8:28, emphasis mine).

In other words, you can release the insecurities that cause you to want to be in control because the God of the universe is in control, every time and all the time, and He actually causes all things to work together *for good* to those who love Him, to those who are called according to His purpose (the elect). Rest assured that He would do a much finer job that you could ever do, even at your best!

10. *Striving to "win the world for Jesus" need no longer be a stressor for you* because God has not only predetermined who His

elect are, but He has also called them unto Himself, justified them, and glorified them, as is evidenced by this: "For whom He foreknew, He also predestined to become conformed to the image of His Son, that He might be the first-born among many brethren; and whom He predestined, these He also *called*, and whom He called, these He also *justified*, and whom He justified, these He also *glorified*" (Romans 8:29–30, emphasis mine).

In other words, the burden of evangelism need no longer rest upon your shoulders! Does this mean you should not pray for the lost, minister to the lost, or witness to the lost or preach to the lost? May it never be! How shall we who have been foreknown, predestined, called, justified, and glorified do anything other than pray, minister, witness, and preach? Even so, God has chosen to shoulder the burden of evangelism; however, in His outrageous mercy and grace, He has also chosen to allow us to participate with Him through our prayers, our ministry, our witness, and yes, even our preaching, as foolish as it might be. The truth is this: He could do a much better job without our being involved, but then, He is a loving Father who takes great pleasure in allowing us to participate with Him, thereby helping us grow unto full stature. Just remember: He shoulders the burden, if there is a burden to shoulder.

11. *Striving to gain the approval of others need no longer be a stressor for you* because God has chosen to lavish His own approval upon you in the person of Jesus, as is evidenced by this: "You were bought with a price; do not become slaves of men" (1 Corinthians 7:23).

In other words, when you seek to gain the approval of others, you will inevitably become their slave because you allow them to control your life—what you wear, where you go, how you speak, where you sit, what automobile you drive, etc. Fortunately, God refuses to be controlled, and He refuses to compete; consequently, out of His great love and acceptance for you in Jesus, He bought you off the slave block, even the slave block of trying to get the approval of others, and He set you free to find your satisfaction in Him.

12. *Striving to deal with feelings of guilt that stem from past sins need no longer be a stressor for you* because Jesus provided the perfect sacrifice for our sins, one that left us without a sin consciousness. This is the evidence: "For the Law, since it has only a shadow of the good things to come and not the very form of things, can never by the same sacrifices year by year, which they offer continually, make perfect those who draw near. Otherwise, would they not have ceased to be offered because the worshippers, having once been cleansed, would no longer have had consciousness of sins? But in those sacrifices, there is a reminder of sins year by year" (Hebrews 10:1–3).

In other words, the evidence that the Day of Atonement was ineffective was this: in each of those sacrifices, there was a reminder of sins year by year (i.e., they left the worshippers very conscious of their sin and therefore heavy-laden with feelings of guilt). On the other hand, the evidence that Jesus's sacrifice was/is effective is this: His sacrifice was a once-for-all-time-sacrifice that completely removed our sins and therefore left us without as much as a hint of sin consciousness—guilt free! You are now free to focus on His righteousness.

13. *Striving to die to self need no longer be a stressor for you* because that death took place when you were crucified in Jesus, as is

evidenced by these passages: (1) "I have been crucified with Christ; and it is no longer I who live, but Christ lives in me; and the life which I now live in the flesh I live by faith in the Son of God, who loved me, and delivered Himself up for me" (Galatians 2:20). (2) "Or do you not know that all of us who have been baptized into Christ Jesus have been baptized into His death?" (Romans 6:3).

In other words, you no longer have to waste your energy trying to kill your old self (Adamic self) because God accomplished that through the death of Jesus. Those who would have you believe that you must die daily to self are simply misinformed, albeit probably well intentioned. To be sure, as a believer, you must reckon (consider) daily that your old man has died and that your new life is hidden with Christ in God. Otherwise, you will live as if you are yet alive in Adam rather than alive in Christ. "For you have died and your life is hidden with Christ in God" (Colossians 3:3).

As I see it you have two choices: (1) you can reject what the scriptures clearly teach and continue trying to kill your old self, or (2) you can accept what the scriptures clearly teach and reckon (consider) your old Adamic self dead— graveyard dead—and your new-creation-self alive in Christ Jesus—spiritually alive. The latter brings victorious living; the former brings defeat.

14. *Pursuing mere happiness need no longer be a stressor for you* because God has a higher dream for your life, as is evidenced by this: "But whatever things were gain to me, those things I have counted as loss for the sake of Christ. More than that, I count all things to be loss in view of the surpassing value of knowing Christ Jesus my Lord, for whom I have suffered the loss of all things, and count them but rubbish

in order that I may gain Christ, and may be found in Him, not having a righteousness of my own derived from the Law, but that which is through faith in Christ, the righteousness which comes from God on the basis of faith, that I may know Him, and the power of His resurrection and the fellowship of His sufferings, being conformed to His death; in order that I may attain to the resurrection from the dead" (Philippians 3:7–11).

In other words, as Paul obviously knew, there is much more for the Christian than mere happiness, yet we seem to desire it above all else. According to Paul's own testimony, nothing could be compared to knowing Christ, even his being a Pharisee. In the end, the things he believed would bring him happiness were, to use his words, dung. This was especially true in view of the surpassing value of God's higher dream for his life—finding ultimate pleasure in Jesus. The problem for us, however, is this: God's dream for us (that we find ultimate pleasure in Jesus) requires that we endure adversity and suffering, even the loss of all things, especially selfish ambitions. Although we fight against adversity, suffering, and loss, God, in His incredible grace and mercy, places them in our lives to cause us to desire Jesus above all else and to thereby find ultimate pleasure in Him. I might add this: When you finally find ultimate pleasure in Jesus, all the happiness in the world pales in significance.

15. *Striving to have enough faith to "get the job done" need no longer be a stressor for you* because "getting the job done" is not dependent upon your faith but upon the faithfulness of His sovereign will, as is evidenced by this: "But if God so arrays the grass of the field, which is alive today and tomorrow is thrown into the furnace, will He not much more do so for you, O men of little faith? Do not be anxious

then, saying, 'What shall we eat?' or 'What shall we drink?' Or 'With what shall we clothe ourselves?' For all these things the Gentiles seek; for your heavenly Father knows that you need all these things. But seek first His kingdom and His righteousness; and all these things will be added to you. Therefore, do not be anxious for tomorrow; for tomorrow will care for itself. Each day has enough trouble of its own" (Matthew 6:30–34).

In other words, the key to getting the job done is not your faith, but the faithfulness of God's sovereign will. Notice what He said: "Will He not much more do so for you, O men of little faith?" Does this mean faith is a nonessential part of the Christian life? May it never be! How shall we, for whom God graciously and lavishly provides, do anything but place our faith and trust in Him? The truth is, *without faith it is impossible to please Him* (Hebrews 11:6), but remember that it is His faith working in us that pleases Him, and His faith is His gift to us, even saving faith. "For by grace you have been saved through faith; and that not of yourselves, it is the gift of God" (Ephesians 2:8). You can rest assured that God will provide you with enough of His faith to get any job done that He wants done, and you can also rest assured that you could never work up that faith, regardless of how hard you might try. If you could, then you would have something about which you could boast, and God will simply not allow you to boast in yourself.

16. *Worrying yourself sick trying to avoid the sin for which there is no forgiveness need no longer be a stressor for you* because, as a believer, there is no sin for which there is no forgiveness, as is evidenced by these passages: (1) "But when Christ appeared as a high priest of the good things to come, He entered through the greater and more perfect tabernacle,

not made with hands, that is to say, not of this creation; and not through the blood of goats and calves, but through His own blood, He entered the holy place once for all, having obtained eternal redemption. For if the blood of goats and bulls and the ashes of a heifer sprinkling those who have been defiled, sanctify for the cleansing of the flesh, how much more will the blood of Christ, who through the eternal Spirit offered Himself without blemish to God, cleanse your conscience from dead works to serve the living God? And for this reason He is the mediator of a new covenant, in order that since a death has taken place for the redemption of the transgressions that were committed under the first covenant, those who have been called may receive the promise of the eternal inheritance" (Hebrews 9:11–15, emphasis mine). *(2)* "No one who is born of God practices sin, because His seed abides in him; and he cannot sin, because he is born of God" (1 John 3:9, emphasis mine).

In other words, the key to being eternally forgiven and to receiving eternal life lies not within your performance but within God's specific call, not to mention that the sins of new covenant participants have been dealt with, not by the blood of bulls and goats but by the blood of Jesus. Then there is the obvious: Jesus is the mediator of the new covenant, not Moses! Finally—and John makes this abundantly clear— the one who is born of God cannot sin because he is born of God! As you can see, this places the believer in a very safe place, far removed from the possibility of committing a sin for which there is no forgiveness. Woe be unto the lost man who commits such a sin, as he has no hope!

Now I realize that some of these benefits and blessings are the very things for which you have been taught to strive; in fact, striving for them has been the pursuit of your Christian life. If the truth be known, your maturity as a Christian has been based on the success of your striving to gain these very things.

All I can tell you is this: the more you embrace the gospel of the grace of God, the more you will embrace His graciousness toward you. If the scriptures are true, and I believe they are, then if you are one of God's children, He has made you a joint-heir with Jesus. You are the recipient of one incredible inheritance.

16

THE CHALLENGE

Truly, truly, I say to you, you seek Me, not because you saw signs, but because you ate of the loaves, and were filled. Do not work for the food which perishes, but for the food which endures to eternal life, which the Son of Man shall give to you, for on Him the Father, even God, has set His seal. They said therefore to Him "What shall we do, that we may work the works of God?" Jesus answered and said to them, "This is the work of God, that you believe in Him whom He has sent." (Jesus: John 6:26–29)

17

THE BENEDICTION

Praise the Lord!
Praise God in His sanctuary;
Praise Him in His mighty expanse.
Praise him for His mighty deeds;
Praise Him according to His excellent greatness.
Praise Him with the trumpet sound;
Praise Him with harp and lyre.
Praise Him with timbrel and dancing;
Praise him with stringed instruments and pipe.
Praise Him with loud cymbals;
Praise Him with resounding cymbals.
Let everything that has breath praise the Lord.
Praise the Lord.

—Psalm 150

18

CLOSING COMMENTS

In my opinion, it goes without saying that, left to himself, man will never believe the gospel message; it is simply too farfetched. Think about it. This Spirit, who calls Himself God, claims to have stood on the canopy of nothing and created everything—the universe and everything it contains. This One, who calls Himself God, also claims to have left heaven to become a man in the person of His only begotten Son, Jesus, who, according to Him, lived some thirty-three years in the land called Israel. He also claims that this Son, Jesus, was born of the virgin womb of a woman named Mary.

Furthermore, He claims this Son came into the world to live among men and eventually to die on a cross to save His people from their sins and to give them eternal life. As if that were not enough, He also claims that this Son was buried in a borrowed tomb, where He remained for only three days and was then raised from the dead.

To add insult to injury, He claims this resurrected Son walked among the people of Israel for forty days after His resurrection, clearly revealing Himself to many of them. Then the icing on the cake: He claims this Son actually ascended back to heaven, thereby returning to His Father, where He now sits at His right hand. Then to top it all off, He claims this Son will return to the earth for His bride and take her back with Him to live forever in the celestial city He calls the New Jerusalem.

Now you tell me, who in the wide world would ever believe this unbelievable story? I will answer my own question: only those to whom He gives the faith to believe this story will believe it, and I might add, every one of them will believe it, and theirs is eternal life—a gift of lavish grace indeed.

It is my sincere prayer that the hours I have spent putting together my perspective of the gospel—*Honey from the Rock: A Study of the Gospel of Grace*—will not have been spent in vain. If you are reading this, please know I have already prayed that God has motivated your heart to press on in your passion to know Him whom to know is eternal life.

May the love of God constrain you; may the joy of the Lord be your strength; and may the peace that passes all understanding be yours in fullest measure. Amen.

BIBLIOGRAPHY

Barnes, M. Craig. *Searching for Home: Spirituality for Restless Souls.* Grand Rapids, MI: Brazos Press, 2003.

Beumer, Juren. *Henri Nouwen: A Restless Seeking for God.* New York: Crossroads Publishing, 1990.

Boettner, Loraine. *The Reformed Doctrine of Predestination.* Phillipsburg, NJ: Presbyterian and Reformed Publishing Company, 1932.

Boice, James Montgomery. *Romans Volume 2: The Reign of Grace—Romans 5–8.* Grand Rapids, MI: Baker Book House, 1992.

Calvin, John. *Institutes of the Christian Religion.* Edited by John T. McNeil. Translated by Ford Lewis Battles. Philadelphia: Westminister, 1960.

Capon, Robert Farrar. *The Mystery of Christ: and Why We Don't Get It.* Grand Rapids, MI: William B. Eerdmans Publishing Company, 1993.

Horton, Michael Scott. *A Better Way: Rediscovering the Drama of God-Centered Worship.* Grand Rapids, MI: Baker Books, 2002.

Horton, Michael Scott, *We Believe: Recovering the Essentials of the Apostle's Creed.* Nashville, TN: Word Publishing, 1998.

Jones, D. Martyn-Lloyd. *God's Ultimate Purpose: An Exposition of Ephesians.* Grand Rapids, MI: Baker Book House, 1978.

Jones, D. Martyn-Lloyd. *God's Way of Reconciliation: Studies in Ephesians Chapter 2.* Grand Rapids, MI: Baker Book House, 1972.

MacArthur, John F. *The MacArthur New Testament Commentary: Hebrews.* Chicago: The Moody Bible Institute of Chicago, 1983.

McNeely, Jim. *The Romance of Grace.* Seattle: Vox Dei, 2013.

Peterson, Eugene H. *The Message.* Colorado Springs, CO: Navpress, 2002.

Smith, Malcolm. *The Power of the Blood Covenant.* Tulsa, OK: Harrison House, 2002.

ANSWER SHEET

Creation

1. *Describe how things were for Adam and Eve as they lived in the garden, before the fall.* Man was created in the image of the Father, Son, and Holy Spirit (Genesis 1:26), according to their likeness (Genesis 1:26), with God's stamp of approval placed upon them (Genesis 1:31)—*man in perfect relationship with God*! They had no sin, no shame, no hiding, and no reason to hide; perfect, beautiful intimacy with the Father and with the Son and with the Holy Spirit!

2. *Why is it critically important that you accept the fact of creation?* If you cannot accept the fact that God literally created *everything* and that He did so from absolutely *nothing*, then sadly, you will be unable to accept the one, true gospel—the gospel of the grace of God.

3. *Which is the greater miracle, the miracle of the physical creation or the miracle of the new creation?* The miracle of the new creation is the story of God doing an even greater miracle than the miracle of physical creation. It is the story of Him creating from nothing a *new creation in Christ Jesus*!

4. *When did the new creation's existence begin?* When the Word of God spoke it into existence—from the foundation of the world. "For you have been born again not of seed which is perishable but imperishable, that is, through the living and abiding *word*

of God" (1 Peter 1:23, emphasis mine). "He finished His works from the foundation of the world" (Hebrews 4:3b).

First Adam, First Man

1. *Why do you suppose we know so little about God?* He designed it so; after all, it was His decision that He would be the Father and we would be the children. He had a committee meeting with Himself (Father, Son, and Holy Spirit) and decided He would be the potter and we would be the clay.

2. *Thankfully, God chose to make two things about Himself very clear. What were they?* "And we have come to know and have believed the love which God has for us. *God is love,* and the one who abides in love abides in God, and God abides in Him" (1 John 4:16, emphasis mine). "*Holy, Holy, Holy* is the Lord of hosts" (Isaiah 6:3, emphasis mine).

3. *I indicated we have a minor problem with God being love. What is it?* It is very difficult to grasp the concept of love because it is so very slippery. For example, one might say, "I love fried chicken." Another might say, "I love deer hunting." Another might say, "I love my mother." One might even say, "I love my enemies." Someone might dare even to say, "I love sinners." One would surely say, "I love my wife!" In addition, let us not forget there would be those brave souls who would say, "I love God!" To be sure, there would be the few who would have the courage to say, "God loves me!" As you can see, in each of these examples, the word *love* is very slippery.

4. *I indicated that we have a minor problem with God being holy. What is it?* We know less about holiness than we do about love! On one hand, what we have seen done in the name of love has so distorted our concept of love that most of us run from whatever it is; on the other hand, holiness is so foreign to us that, for the most part, we do not have a clue.

5. *How can we define love?* We can say that whatever else love might be, it is first and foremost the stuff of which God is made, and we can say He demonstrated it to us on the cross when, "He did not spare His own Son, but delivered Him up for us" (Romans 8:32). "Love never fails" (1 Corinthians 13:8)!

6. *How can we define holiness?* We can say that whatever else holiness might be, it is first and foremost the stuff of which God is made, and we can say He demonstrated His holiness to us when He required that His Son bear our sins in His body on the cross. "And He Himself bore our sins in His body on the cross, that we might die to sin and live to righteousness; for by His wounds you were healed" (1 Peter 2:24). *Holiness never compromises!*

7. *What would the God of love and holiness do with His love and holiness?* He would create man and place within him the need for love and holiness, and furthermore, He would place His creation in an environment that was drenched with love and holiness.

8. *Why would this God of love and holiness do the above-mentioned things?* On one hand, He would place the need for love within His creation because He would want him to be eager to receive His love, to be the recipient of who He is. On the other hand, He would place him in an environment of holiness because He would not want him exposed to sin! Ultimately, of course, He would do both of these to glorify Himself!

9. *Why did God choose to bring Eve on the scene?* Thankfully, God saw that it was not good for man to live alone! Then the Lord God said, "It is not good for the man to be alone; I will make him a helper suitable for him" (Genesis 2:18).

The Fall

1. *Was this first Adam, first man really complete?* No! It is important for you to realize that *at this point*, neither Adam nor Eve had eaten from the tree of life—Jesus—or from the tree of knowledge

of good and evil. Even though they lived in the perfect garden, completeness required the tree of life.

2. *What indicated that Adam and Eve made the only free choice man ever made?* It is important for you to realize that *at this point,* neither Adam nor Eve had eaten from the tree of life—Jesus— or from the tree of knowledge of good and evil—religion and death—which just might indicate they were about to make the only free choice man has ever made.

3. *Explain why #2 is true.* They were under the influence of neither tree.

4. *What choice did Adam make?* Adam chose to do what every man would choose to do when he has a free choice—make the wrong choice! He chose to do the *only* thing God told him not to do! He ate the fruit of the tree of knowledge of good and evil. He made the very same choice each one of us would have made had we been there (and we were)—the wrong choice!

5. *When Adam made the choice to eat of the forbidden tree, what other choice did he make?* He rejected the tree of life!

6. *Other than God, what gave Adam the toughest problem?* The thou-shalt-not rule.

7. *What was the serpent's purpose in tempting Eve?* He wanted Eve to begin questioning what God had said so she would become confused about it. After all, he is the author of confusion!

8. *I indicated that the serpent had accomplished his first mission very quickly. What was it?* Deception and confusion! He was using that good, holy, and righteous No Trespassing sign (the thou-shalt-not rule) to bring about deception and confusion!

9. *What would prove to be the serpent's long-term course of action?* His using that which is good, holy, and righteous (the law) to bring about deception and confusion, and ultimately death would prove to be his long-term course of action (see Romans 7:7–14).

10. *In the serpent's no-holds-barred, all-out mission to deceive Eve, what was his purpose?* He was on a no-holds-barred, all-out mission to deceive her just enough to get her to take one bite of

the fruit from the forbidden tree, and he was because he knew *that* would be all it would take.

11. *What was the immediate consequence of Adam's and Eve's eyes being opened?* "Then the eyes of both of them were opened, and *they knew that they were naked*" (Genesis 3:7, emphasis mine).

12. *What was their response to seeing their nakedness?* Shame. "And they sewed fig leaves together and made themselves loin coverings" (Genesis 3:7).

13. *I indicated that Adam and Eve tried to cover their private parts with the fig leaves. Apply this to your life.* How many times have you tried to cover your private parts, the secrets you keep hidden deep within, with some form of fig leaf? The sad truth is this: when we try to hide, we only breed more shame. Secrets always breed shame—always!

14. *What was God's reason for the thou-shalt-not rule—the No Trespassing sign?* He knew there was no way they would obey it, and He also knew (in the big scheme of things) their inability to obey this No Trespassing sign would be the only thing that would ultimately drive them to tree of life. Of course, their immediate concern was to rid themselves of this terrible shame they were experiencing; however, they were short on thread, and the fig leaves were too small and too thin! His immediate concern was for them to eat of the tree of life!

15. *How could something that had so perfectly blended into God's creation that it went unnoticed become something so painfully and shamefully obvious?* It did because the road to independence from God is filled with potholes of pain and shame.

16. *When I experience shame, what strong and convincing message does it send to me?* Interestingly, shame has to do with my perception of who I am, not what I do. When I experience shame, it sends this strong and convincing message to me: You are inadequate, unworthy, useless, inferior, guilty, dumb, stupid, unloved, and unlovely! The moment I believe it, I allow shame to determine my identity. Unfortunately, shame breeds more shame, which serves only to reinforce my perceived identity.

17. *Why did Adam and Eve try to hide from God?* They had disobeyed Him!

18. *In this hide-and-go-seek game, who was the seeker?* God—always! "There in none who seeks for God" (Romans 3:11b).

19. *How did Adam attempt to exonerate himself before God?* "The woman whom Thou gavest to be with me, she gave me from the tree, and I ate" (Genesis 3:12).

20. *What was Eve's defense?* "Then the Lord God said to the woman, 'What is this you have done?' And the woman said, 'The serpent deceived me and I ate'" (Genesis 3:13).

21. *What was the first indication of light in this entire dark tragedy?* "And the woman said, 'the serpent deceived me and I ate'" (Genesis 3:13).

22. *Who led Eve out of the darkness of her deception?* God and God alone brought her out of the darkness of deception! His question was the secret: "What is this you have done?" (Genesis 3:13). I might add this: It is always God and God alone who brings us out of the darkness of deception.

23. *What was the consequence of the fall?* The first Adam, first man fell by making the wrong choice; consequently, his perfect relationship with God was destroyed and man was left incomplete and on his own!

The Consequences for Their Disobedience

1. *Specifically, what was the* consequence *of Eve's sin? Is that consequence applicable today?* "I will greatly multiply your pain in childbirth, in pain you shall bring forth children; yet your desire shall be for your husband, and he shall rule over you" (Genesis 3:16)

2. *Specifically, what was the* consequence *of Adam's sin? Is that consequence applicable today?* "Cursed is the ground because of you; in toil you shall eat of it all the days of your life. Both thorns

and thistles it shall grow for you; and you shall eat the plants of the field; by the sweat of your face you shall eat bread, till you return to the ground, because from it you were taken; for you are dust, and to dust you shall return" (Genesis 3:17-19)

3. *Is there a difference between the consequences for sin and the punishment for sin?* Very much so! The consequences are corrective whereas the punishment is death.

The Punishment for Their Disobedience

1. *God punished the serpent in a very specific way. What was it?* "And the Lord God said to the serpent, 'Because you have done this, cursed are you more than all cattle, and more than every beast of the field; on your belly shall you go, and dust shall you eat all the days of your life; and I will put enmity between you and the woman, and between your seed and her seed; He shall bruise you on your head, and you shall bruise him on the heel'" (Genesis 3:14–15).

2. *God punished Eve in a very particular way. What was it?* "To the woman He said, 'I will greatly multiply your pain in childbirth, in pain you shall bring forth children; yet your desire shall be for your husband, and he shall rule over you'" (Genesis 3:16).

3. *God punished Adam in a very particular way. What was it?* "Then to Adam He said, 'Because you have listened to the voice of your wife, and have eaten from the tree about which I commanded you, saying, 'You shall not eat from it'; cursed is the ground because of you; in toil you shall eat of it all the days of your life. Both thorns and thistles it shall grow for you; and you shall eat the plants of the field; by the sweat of your face you shall eat bread, till you return to the ground, because from it you were taken; for you are dust, and to dust you shall return'" (Genesis 3:17–19).

4. *Although God had a very particular and separate punishment for Adam and Eve, He also punished them together with the same*

punishment. What was it? "Then the Lord God said, 'Behold, the man has become like one of Us, knowing good and evil; and now, lest he stretch out his hand, and take also from the tree of life, and eat, and live forever'—therefore the Lord sent him out from the garden of Eden, to cultivate the ground from which he was taken. So He drove the man out; and at the east of the Garden of Eden He stationed the cherubim, and the flaming sword which turned every direction, to guard the way to the tree of life" (Genesis 3:22–24).

5. *What did God do concerning the fig leaves just before He sent Adam and Eve out of the garden?* "And the Lord God made garments of skin for Adam and his wife, and clothed them" (Genesis 3:21).

6. *What might be the significance of these garments of skin?* We have an animal sacrificed, blood spilled, and a covering made! This might possibly mean that where sin increases, grace abounds even more. This just might mean that God forgave Adam and Eve. It is possible that this sacrificed animal, this shed blood, and this covering of skin were a shadow of something *good* to come.

7. *Did God punish all of humanity because Adam sinned?* Yes!

8. *How did God punish the rest of humanity?* "For the wages of sin is death" (Romans 6:23a).

9. *Humanity's problem was twofold. Explain.* (1) We are Adam's offspring (he was the first man, first Adam, remember?) and therefore, we have his sinful, depraved seed in us. (2) We have offended *the holy God*! When all is said and done, this is really our most serious problem, and we are helpless and hopeless to solve it. "Therefore, just as through one man sin entered into the world, and death through sin, and so death spread to all men, *because all sinned*" (Romans 5:12, emphasis mine). "For *all have sinned* and *fall short of the glory of God*" (Romans 3:23, emphasis mine).

10. *What is God's standard for membership into His redeemed, justified, perfect family?* His standard for membership is very high—perfection. "Therefore you are to be perfect, as your heavenly Father is perfect" (Matthew 5:48).

11. *How did Abel manage to meet God's standard of perfection?* To be sure, Abel, like his parents, did not reach God standard of perfection. Obviously, God's acceptance of him had to do with the offering he offered to God, not a grain offering but from the firstlings of his flock. Abel's offering had to do with sacrificing animals; Cain's did not. "So it came about in the course of time that Cain brought an offering to the Lord of the fruit of the ground. And Abel, on his part also brought of the firstling of his flock and of their fat portions" (Genesis 4:3–4a).

12. *What seems to be the only common denominator of those who have gained membership into God's family?* The only common denominator I have been able to find is this: not one of those in His family deserved to be there.

13. *How did sin enter into the world and thereby defile everyone?* "Therefore, just as through one man sin entered into the world, and death through sin, and so death spread to all men, because all sinned" (Romans 5:12).

14. *What about the condition of those who lived between Moses and the law and who therefore did not sin in the way Adam sinned?* "Nevertheless death reigned from Adam until Moses, even over those who had not sinned in the likeness of the offense of Adam, who is a type of Him who was to come" (Romans 5:14).

Two Families: Adam's and God's

1. *How did we enter into this world?* We entered into this world hopelessly lost, sinfully depraved, separated from God, and on our way to hell.

2. *How did the way we entered into the world affect God's love for us?* Fortunately, none of this changed the love of God or the holiness of God. In spite of our having been born in Adam and our resulting depravity, He continues to be the same loving and holy God He has always been, even toward us. This becomes obvious

as we realize the significance of His having chosen to do for some of us what none of us could have done for ourselves—redeem us and bring us home.

3. *Into which family were you physically born—Adam's family or God's family?* Adam's family!

4. *I indicated that God has always been intent on redeeming some of us from the terrible fall—delivering us from Adam's family and transferring us to God's family. What text verifies this?* "And Isaiah cries out concerning Israel, 'Though the number of the sons of Israel be as the sand of the sea, it is the remnant that will be saved'" (Romans 9:21).

5. *Who did God set in place as the head of His family?* Jesus, the last Adam, second man.

6. *What ties did this last Adam, second man have with the first Adam, first man?* None! Jesus was born of the seed of God, not the seed of Adam.

7. *As you remember, God created Adam from the dust of the earth and breathed into him the breath of life. How did God arrange for Jesus's entrance on the earth?* This last Adam, second man (Jesus) was conceived by the Holy Spirit as the result of the imperishable seed of the Word of God entering the virgin womb of Mary. Jesus (last Adam, second man) was born, therefore, of God's seed and consequently, free from the seed of Adam.

8. *Why did God identify Jesus as the last Adam, second man?* God identified Jesus as the second man because he is the man (human) God designated to be the head of the second significant family—His chosen family. God identified Jesus as the last Adam because there would never be the need for another Adam.

9. *I indicated there were two significant things one should remember about this last Adam, second man. What were they?* (1) He existed long before the first Adam, first-man ever thought about existing. (2) He was born of a woman and born under the law.

10. *Why are these things significant?* (1) They prove the eternal nature of Jesus. "Thou, Lord, in the beginning didst lay the foundation

of the earth, and the heavens are the works of Thy hands; they will perish, but thou remainest; and they all will become old as a garment, and as a mantle Thou wilt roll them up, as a garment they will also be changed. But Thou art the same, and Thy years will not come to an end" (Hebrews 1:10–12). "Jesus Christ is the same yesterday and today, yes and forever" (Hebrews 13:8). (2) They prove Jesus's ability not only to redeem us but also to release us from the law. "But when the fullness of the time came, God sent forth His Son, born of a woman, born under the Law, in order that He might redeem those who were under the Law, that we might receive the adoption as sons" (Galatians 3:4–5).

11. *Do the scriptures indicate that the Gentiles will be able to enter God's family?* Yes. *How?* "You will say to me then, 'Branches were broken off so that I might be grafted in.' Quite right, they were broken off for their unbelief, but you stand by your faith" (Romans 11:19–20a). "For if you were cut off from what is by nature a wild olive tree, and were grafted contrary to nature into a cultivated olive tree, how much more shall these who are the natural branches be grafted into their own olive tree?" (Romans 11:24).

12. *How are the traits of God's family different from the traits of Adam's family?* Fortunately, the traits of God's family are significantly different from those of Adam's family! Every member of God's family is born, as was Jesus, free from Adam's seed—a saint, not a sinner; a pleasure to God, not offensive to Him; in perfect relationship with Him, not in a broken relationship with Him; having hope, not hopeless; freed from sin, not enslaved to sin; enslaved to righteousness, not free from righteousness; destined for heaven, not doomed to hell; free from the guilt of sin, not condemned; free from the penalty of sin, not facing the wages of sin—to mention a few.

13. *One would think all people would be keenly interested in finding out just how they might leave Adam's sinful, depraved family and enter into God's redeemed, righteous family; however, this is not the case. Why?* The gospel is offensive—very offensive, so much

so that only the Holy Spirit can make it attractive! If you do not believe this, go back and revisit the Jews' response to it. Why, the scribes and Pharisees labeled Jesus as a blasphemer! "And the scribes and the Pharisees began to reason saying, 'Who is this man who speaks blasphemies? Who can forgive sins, but God alone?'" (Luke 5:21).

14. *Who was one of the first to whom God gave membership into His family?* Abel.

15. *How does God determine whom He will allow into His family?* He does so after the counsel of His will. "Also we have obtained an inheritance, having been predestined according to His purpose who works all things *after the counsel of His will*, to the end that we who were the first to hope in Christ should be to the praise of His glory" (Ephesians 1:11–12, emphasis mine).

16. *If you have an inclination for Jesus, I indicated you were probably already asking this question: How can I leave Adam's family and enter God's family? How can you?* Well, the truth is this: If you have an inclination for Jesus, He has already delivered you from the kingdom of darkness—Adam's sinful, depraved family—and transferred you to the kingdom of His dear Son—God's family! My dear friend, you are already home—truly home.

17. *List three of the personal dynamics of the incredible miracle of being delivered from the kingdom of darkness and transferred to the kingdom of God's dear Son, that is, being delivered from Adam's family and transferred to the family of God.* (1) You would do well to realize that you did not leave Adam's family on your own, and neither did you enter God's family on your own; you simply cannot save yourself. (2) It would behoove you to realize that this miracle is a matter of grace (i.e., you cannot and do not and will not deserve it—period). (3) It would be very beneficial if you would accept the fact that this new life is a life of faith—relentless trust in the finished work of Jesus.

18. *What was Jesus's response to Nicodemus's question, "How can a man be born when he is old?"* "Truly, truly, I say to you, unless one is

born of water and the Spirit, he cannot enter into the kingdom of God. That which is born of the flesh is flesh, and that which is born of the Spirit is spirit. Do not marvel that I said to you, 'You must be born again.' The wind blows where it wishes and you hear the sound of it, but do not know where it comes from and where it is going; so is everyone who is born of the Spirit" (John 3:1–8).

19. *Jesus clearly said to Nicodemus, "Unless one is born again he cannot see the kingdom of God." Therefore, we must take this seriously. Let me ask the logical question: How is one born again?* As Paul tells us in Romans 6, it is all the work of God, which is probably why Jesus's answer to Nicodemus was rather "windy." "Or do you not know that *all of us who have been baptized into Christ Jesus* have been *baptized into His death*? Therefore, we have been *buried with Him* through baptism into death, in order that as Christ was raised from the dead through the glory of the Father, so we too might walk in newness of life. For if we have become united with Him in the likeness of His death, certainly we shall be also in *the likeness of His resurrection*, knowing this, that *our old self was crucified with Him*, that our body of sin might be done away with, that we should no longer be slaves to sin; for he who has died is freed from sin" (Romans 6:3–6, emphasis mine).

20. *What is the significance of your having been baptized into Jesus' death?* The old, Adamic man that I was via Adam is dead—graveyard dead. I no longer have to purpose to kill him.

21. *What is the significance of your having been buried with Jesus?* I no longer have to deal with that old, Adamic man because he is completely out of the way.

22. *What is the significance of your having been united with Christ in the likeness of His resurrection?* I am a new creation in Him, living in the resurrection of Jesus!

23. *What are some of the benefits of your having been released from Adam's family and born again with the seed of God into God's redeemed family?* (1) We walk in newness of life. (2) Our bodies of

sin have been done away with. (3) We are no longer slaves to sin. (4) We are free from sin because we are dead to sin. (5) We are alive to God. (6) We are no longer under the law's jurisdiction. (7) We live under grace. (8) We are slaves of righteousness. (9) We are sanctified. (10) We have eternal life.

24. *Are you in Adam, or are you in Christ?*

God's Treatment of Our Sins

1. *What is the usual and pat answer to this question: What happened at the cross?* Jesus died for my sins so I can go to heaven when I die.

2. *There are two sides to the proverbial coin concerning what happened at the cross. What are they?* (1) How Jesus dealt with the old, Adamic man. (2) How Jesus dealt with sins.

3. *Jesus made five significant accomplishments concerning our sins through His vicarious death on the cross. What are they?* (1) He bore our sins in His body. (2) God declared Him guilty of our sins. (3) God punished Him for our sins to the full requirement of the law. (4) He became our scapegoat and took our sins away—as far away as the east is from the west. (5) God declared us forgiven.

4. *What role does each of the following play in the life of a Christian: confession, repentance, and asking for forgiveness?* Confession is by definition agreeing with God and certainly, we want to do just that; however, to confess sins for which Jesus has already paid the penalty is to disagree with God. Furthermore, to repent of sins for which Jesus has already paid the penalty is also to disagree with God. Finally, asking God for His forgiveness for sins for which Jesus has already paid the penalty is again to disagree with God. So let us see if we can agree with Him rather than disagree with Him.

5. *Explain how God's treatment of our sin was all about God's doing, not ours.* (1) God took the initiative to begin a new, perfect family and to place Jesus at its head. (2) God took the initiative

to crucify our Adamic man. (3) God took the initiative to bury that Adamic man. (4) God took the initiative to raise a new creation in Christ Jesus. (5) God took the initiative to place His perfect, imperishable seed in this new creation. (6) God declared that in Christ, we have met His standard for membership into His perfect, redeemed family. (7) God took the initiative to invite you draw near to Him and to sit at His right hand in Jesus.

The Covenant of Law

1. *What the phrase* performance-based acceptance *mean?* Performance-based acceptance is attempting to gain God's acceptance by keeping the Ten Commandments and the other myriad of laws the church and significant others impose.
2. *Define Christianity.* Christianity is an intimate love relationship with Jesus that thrills the heart of God.
3. *Which is the most famous of God's covenants?* The most famous of God's covenants is the covenant He made with the Israelites after He had set them free from Egyptian slavery—the covenant of law.
4. *What was God's promise in this covenant He made with the Israelites?* If you obey My voice and keep My law, then I will bless you; if you fail to obey My voice and to keep My law, then I will curse you.
5. *Upon whose shoulders did the success of the covenant of law rest?* The Israelites.
6. *What was the law the Israelites promised to obey?* The Ten Commandments.
7. *List the Ten Commandments:* (1) You shall have no other gods before Me. (2) You shall not make for yourself an idol, or any likeness of what is in the heaven above or on the earth beneath or in the water under the earth. (3) You shall not take the name of the Lord your God in vain. (4) Remember the Sabbath day to keep it holy. (5) Honor your father and your mother. (6) You

shall not murder. (7) You shall not commit adultery. (8) You shall not steal. (9) You shall not bear false witness against your neighbor. (10) You shall not covet.

8. *What was the result of Israel's effort to interpret the Ten Commandments?* Many, many more laws.

9. *What is God's standard for obedience?* Perfect obedience! "Therefore you are to be perfect, as your heavenly Father is perfect" (Matthew 5:48).

10. *What is the evidence that many have made the Ten Commandments objects of worship?* By man's continued and futile effort to obtain righteousness by following the Ten Commandments, he has unwittingly made them objects of worship; consequently, they have become one of the "other gods" God clearly warned us, with the first commandment, not to worship.

11. *Did God intend the law to be our means to righteousness?* No!

12. *The scriptures enumerate five reasons as to why God gave the law. What are they?* (1) *To give us knowledge of sin*: "Because by works of the Law no flesh will be justified in His sight; for through the Law comes the knowledge of sin" (Romans 3:20). (2) *To define sin*: "On the contrary, I would not have come to know sin except through the Law; for I would not have known about coveting if the Law had not said, 'YOU SHALL NOT COVET'" (Romans 7:7). (3) *To show us the exceeding sinfulness of sin*: "But sin, taking opportunity through the commandment, produced in me coveting of every kind; for apart from the Law sin is dead" (Romans 7:8). (4) *To give sin its power*: "For apart from the Law, sin is dead (Romans 7:8b); The sting of death is sin, and the power of sin is the law" (1 Corinthians 15:56). (5) *To be a child trainer (tutor) to lead (drive) us to Jesus*: "Therefore the Law has become our tutor to lead us to Christ, that we may be justified by faith" (Galatians 3:24).

13. *How does Paul describe the Ten Commandments?* The law of sin and death (Romans 8:2), the ministry of death, and the ministry of condemnation (2 Corinthians 3).

14. *Give a brief contrast between the covenant of law and the covenant of grace.* The old covenant is a covenant of sin and condemnation, a ministry of death, whereas the new covenant is a covenant of righteousness and life in Christ Jesus, a ministry of the Spirit.

15. *Why does Paul identify the law as being holy, righteous, and good?* He does so because: (1) God is its author; (2) it is an expression of God's character—His holiness; (3) it gives us knowledge of sin; (4) it defines sin for us; (5) it shows us the exceeding sinfulness of sin; (6) it gives sin its power; and therefore, (7) it is a child trainer that leads (drives) us to Jesus.

The Covenant of Grace

1. *Why is the new covenant, the covenant of grace, a new and better covenant?* Unlike the old covenant that was between God and man, this is a covenant made between God and Jesus in our behalf. In other words, the success of the covenant depends upon Jesus, not upon us. He is the guarantee that the relationship will be successful.

2. *What are the specific benefits of the covenant of grace? In the first place,* God wrote His old covenant laws—the Ten Commandments—onto tablets of stone. As you can see, they were carved into stone and therefore could offer no grace to the worshipper. However, God wrote His new covenant laws—love God and love one another (the law of the Spirit of life in Christ Jesus)—upon the hearts and minds of believers, obviously providing for much grace. *In the second place,* the old covenant was a covenant of works and therefore a covenant of mistrust, whereas the new covenant is a covenant of faith and therefore, a covenant of trust. *In the third place,* the old covenant required us to keep the law—perfectly keeping the law. However, in the new covenant, God has released us from the law. *In the fourth and final place,* the old covenant of law always leaves its worshippers with a

consciousness of sin, which, by the way, is the evidence that it does not make its worshippers perfect, whereas through the new covenant of grace, Jesus removes our consciousness of sin and thereby evidences the efficaciousness of His vicarious sacrifice.

3. *What is the heart and essence of new covenant living?* No more sin consciousness!

His Finished Work

1. *When Jesus finished His work, He sat down. Why?* He was finished with His work.
2. *Define "Sabbath rest."* It is that all-important rest God has provided for us through the work God accomplished in Jesus from before the foundation of the world. It is an eternal rest from the fear of losing the most precious gift anyone could ever receive: eternal life. Furthermore, it is an eternal rest from pretending to be someone you are not, from striving to reach an unreachable goal, from our futile attempts at making ourselves acceptable to the God, who said, "Therefore you are to be perfect, as your heavenly Father is perfect" (Matthew 5:48).
3. *Is this rest an essential ingredient in or an addendum to our justification?* No.
4. *Is there something we must do to finish Jesus's work?* No!
5. *Why do so many Christians fall short of entering into this Sabbath rest?* The deceitfulness of sin.
6. *What is the result of believers falling short of this Sabbath rest?* All too soon, they find themselves back in that familiar struggle to become what God has already declared them to be—saints; consequently, they seldom experience the joy and peace and assurance true Christianity offers. They become tired, weary, grumpy, angry, and frustrated in their struggle; at best, they live the life of a modern-day Pharisee.

7. *What is the warning the author gives to his readers concerning this Sabbath rest?* "Therefore, let us fear lest, while a promise remains of entering His rest, any one of you should seem to have come short of it" (Hebrews 3:1).

8. *Every Christian actually lives every moment of every day in the Sabbath rest. True or false? Explain.* This is true because Jesus is the Sabbath rest and we live in Him every moment of every day. There is, however, a vast difference between living in that rest without knowing it (falling short of it) and living in that rest and knowing it (consciously entering into it)!

9. *Describe what the scriptures mean by the "deceitfulness of sin."* When sin convinces you that you will continue to be righteous if you *do not* commit a given act of sin, or when sin convinces you that you will no longer be righteous if you *do* commit a given act of sin, it has demonstrated its deceitfulness. To say that another way, when sin convinces you that *you can achieve* the rest God has provided for you through the finished work of Jesus, it has demonstrated its deceitfulness. Furthermore, when sin convinces you that *you can fail to achieve* this rest and thereby lose your fellowship with God or your relationship with Him, it has demonstrated its deceitfulness.

10. *What does "following this same example of disobedience" mean?* It means doing what Israel did! It is placing your trust in your ability to achieve righteousness rather than placing your trust in Jesus's ability to achieve righteousness for you! It is viewing the Sabbath as a day you are to keep holy rather than viewing it as the person of Jesus, who is holy! It is refusing to accept Him as your Sabbath rest!

11. *How can we recognize one who has truly entered into the Sabbath rest?* "For the one who has entered His rest *has himself also rested* from his works, as God did from His" (Hebrews 4:10, emphasis mine).

12. *Is God in some kind of time crunch regarding evangelism and therefore in need of our help to gather His family together?* No! Somewhere, long before the world ever was, God finished the work that was necessary for the redemption of His elect.

13. *What is the antithesis of rest?* Stress!

Faith without Works

1. *Is it possible for one to have genuine faith in Jesus and in His finished work without doing the good works God prepared beforehand for us?* Absolutely not! These good works are the fruit of faith in Him and in His finished work.
2. *How can we know the works we do are actually good works?* Motivation.
3. *Do our works, whether they are works of the flesh or works of the Spirit (good works), do anything to earn right standing with God?* Absolutely not!
4. *Do our works, whether they are works of the flesh or good works, impress God at all?* Absolutely not!
5. *What must happen before anyone can do the good works God prepared for us?* We must be free from the tyranny of the law.
6. *What is a workaholic?* Someone whose work ethic is based upon fear, not faith.
7. *What motivates a workaholic?* The lack of positive self-image and self-concept.
8. *If fear is motivating us, what kind of works will we inevitably do?* Works of the flesh.

Concerning God's Elect

1. *Why do you think so many people struggle with the terms* choice, election, foreknowledge, *and* predestination? These terms place God where He belongs—above all—and they place man where he belongs—depraved and in need of the Savior.
2. *Did God call all people and then leave the choice to respond positively up to them, or did God only call a particular group of people and*

guarantee their justification? According to the text, God called a particular group of people and justified them.

3. *Did God's prescience determine His choice in election?* No! He saw nothing good in any of us—nothing at all.

4. *Paul tells us in Romans 9 that God shows mercy to whom He chooses to show mercy and He hardens whom He chooses to harden. Is that fair?* Who said God has to be fair?

5. *Do you really want God to be fair?* No! If He were, then none of us would stand a chance.

The Altar Call

1. *In the minds of some, the invitation is all-important. Why?* In their minds, it is the method of drawing in the lost for salvation.

2. *What does God use to draw in sinners other than the obvious—the Holy Spirit?* The foolishness of the message preached.

3. *Why is it a good thing to invite folks to Jesus?* A true believer could do nothing else!

4. *What is the most effective invitation? Explain.* The holy Eucharist! When one of God's elect, who has not yet been made aware that he or she is one of God's elect, is sitting in the congregation being drawn to Jesus through the foolishness of the message preached, the Eucharist becomes quite an attraction! "For as often as you eat this bread and drink the cup, you proclaim the Lord's death until He comes" (1 Corinthians 11:26).

CPSIA information can be obtained at www.ICGtesting.com
Printed in the USA
LVOW12s1622030114

367904LV00001B/2/P